The Business of Quantum Technologies

"This thoughtful, well researched and comprehensively referenced volume on quantum technologies provides an introduction to this mathematically complex subject via the extensive use of business cases and examples of global research collaborations. The authors stress both the exciting economic potential and the implicit threat underlying current programmes, for example in on-line security or in enabling high frequency financial trading. A 'must-read' for policy makers and practitioners alike."

—Sir Peter Williams, *Former Chairman Oxford Instruments and National Physical Laboratory*

"A masterful synthesis of quantum science, technology adoption and business innovation! One of the standout qualities of The Business of Quantum Technologies is its ability to demystify complex concepts like Shor's algorithm and quantum cryptography by employing relatable analogies, straightforward language, and an emphasis on conceptual logic. The other standout feature is the "4V" framework, which guides executives on how to thoughtfully include quantum technologies into their business strategies. This is the much-needed quantum playbook for the sophisticated business executive."

—Sridhar Tayur, *Ford Distinguished Research Chair and University Professor of Operations Management, Quantum Technologies Group, Tepper School of Business, Carnegie Mellon University*

"The book applies business and societal models and frameworks to understand and anticipate the growth trajectory of the quantum technology industry field. The content is insightful, investigating the important interplay between both businesses and governments in promoting this strategic technology."

—Thierry Botter, *Executive Director of the European Quantum Industry Consortium (QuIC)*

"The trauma of the introduction of a radical technology can wipe out the productivity benefits it is supposed to bring. Using well researched examples in quantum technologies—computing, networking, sensing and navigation—the authors of this book visualise a new approach in which firms and policy makers engage much earlier, new companies work alongside established incumbents, and the pioneering products are hybrid solutions created from new and classical devices."

—Roger McKinlay, *Challenge Director Quantum Technologies, Innovate UK*

"Quantum technologies have the potential to transform many areas of science and business, but technology innovation in itself does not guarantee that businesses will benefit from these developments. This book describes work to address this challenge and provides useful insights and concrete recommendations to help ensure the uptake of these transformative technologies. Those involved in business and innovation, wishing to take advantage of these transformative technologies, will find it a valuable resource"

—Dominic O'Brien, *Professor of Engineering Science, Director QCi3 Hub, University of Oxford*

"The Business of Quantum Technologies: From Theory to Innovation Strategy will be a very useful reference for researchers willing to explore research opportunities on the business model and innovative potential of quantum technologies. It will also be useful for CXOs of companies which intend to reap the benefits of quantum technologies for developing new products."

—Atanu Chaudhuri, *Professor of Technology and Operations Management, Durham University Business School, Durham University*

Chander Velu · Keith Norman · Yuzhen Zhu ·
Fathiro Hutama Reksa Putra ·
Christopher Noble

The Business of Quantum Technologies

From Theory to Innovation Strategy

palgrave
macmillan

Chander Velu
Institute for Manufacturing
Department for Engineering
University of Cambridge
Cambridge, UK

Yuzhen Zhu
Norwich Business School
University of East Anglia
Norwich, UK

Christopher Noble
Department of Physics
University of Oxford
Oxford, UK

Keith Norman
Department of Physics
University of Oxford
Oxford, UK

Fathiro Hutama Reksa Putra
Bandung Institute of Technology
Kota Bandung, Indonesia

ISBN 978-3-031-99807-2 ISBN 978-3-031-99808-9 (eBook)
https://doi.org/10.1007/978-3-031-99808-9

This work was supported by the Engineering and Physical Sciences Research Council [grant number EP/R024367/1]

This Palgrave Macmillan imprint is published by the registered company Springer Nature Switzerland AG
The registered company address is: Gewerbestrasse 11, 6330 Cham, Switzerland

Professor [Max] Planck, of Berlin, the famous originator of the Quantum Theory, once remarked to me that in early life he had thought of studying economics, but had found it too difficult! … the amalgam of logic and intuition and the wide knowledge of facts, most of which are not precise, which is required for economic interpretation in its highest form is, quite truly, overwhelmingly difficult for those whose gift mainly consists in the power to imagine and pursue to their furthest points the implications and prior conditions of comparatively simple facts which are known with a high degree of precision. **John Maynard Keynes**

Essays in Biography, edited by Geoffrey Keynes (Rupert Hart-Davis 1933)

The way of progress is neither swift nor easy. **Marie Curie**

Autobiographical Notes: The Story of My Life, 1923, by Marie Curie (Musée Curie 2013)

Anyone who doesn't feel dizzy when trying to understand quantum mechanics, hasn't really understood it. **Niels Bohr**

From correspondence with Tomas Bohr (grandson of Niels Bohr) by recollection of Aage Bohr's (son of Niels Bohr) conversation with Niels Bohr

Preface

The idea for this book germinated from our curiosity about the reasons for the slowdown in productivity growth rates following the emergence of radically new technologies. The productivity slowdown has been evident since the adoption of general purpose technologies that are meant to improve efficiency, such as electric motors and digital computers. Economists have provided various explanations for the productivity paradox. It occurred to us that most of the studies have focused on past technological adoption or current challenges in firms adopting digital technologies to improve performance. Although insightful, these studies observe the facts largely after the event or when the technology is relatively mature, potentially not fully capturing the strategic decision-making process of firms and policy-makers as the technology matures. One of the major gaps in understanding is how firms and policy-makers need to prepare to adopt technologies that are emerging from research in science and engineering, but which are only likely to be adopted in the future. Therefore, we decided to examine innovation related to quantum technologies.

This prompted us at the Institute for Manufacturing, the University of Cambridge Engineering Department, and the Quantum Computing & Simulation Hub, a multi-university research consortium led by the University of Oxford, to explore the business and economic aspects of quantum technologies. We conducted a series of interviews and roundtable discussions with stakeholders across the quantum landscape, including potential users and technology suppliers. Our research highlighted both the opportunities and the challenges of commercialising and scaling up quantum technologies. Business model innovation emerged as a key contributor to solutions to society's challenges, leading to enhanced productivity and economic growth. Our research made us realise that we need to encourage teams of researchers across business, economics, and management to collectively work with scientists and engineers to improve innovation and technology management of quantum technologies, enabling the benefits of quantum technologies to be realised in the near future. We believe it is imperative to conduct the research in "living labs", where managers and researchers are experimenting with quantum technologies and learning to innovate.

The book provides the foundational conceptual knowledge in a field that is rapidly evolving and describes the evolution of quantum technologies that are likely to have significant economic, business, and geopolitical implications. Although we provide a background to the science, we have attempted to write the book with minimal technical terms from quantum mechanics to provide an intuitive explanation to non-specialists. The aim of the book is to highlight the major areas of research in the business application of quantum technologies. It emphasises areas for future research, provides frameworks to better understand how to adopt and integrate quantum technologies in organisations, and outlines the policy issues with respect to quantum technologies. We believe the book will interest undergraduate and graduate students in economics, innovation, and management who wish to familiarise themselves with the key developments in quantum technologies and better understand the business implications. In addition, the book will appeal to reflective senior executives in organisations who want to obtain a deeper understanding of the theory underpinning quantum technology adoption. The United Nations proclaimed 2025 as the International Year of Quantum Science and Technology, and at this important time marking 100 years of quantum science, we hope this book will provide the intellectual foundations for scholars, managers, and policy-makers to work together to enable quantum technologies to address grand societal challenges, while contributing to productivity and economic growth in a responsible and sustainable manner.

Cambridge, UK — Chander Velu
Oxford, UK — Keith Norman
Oxford, UK — Christopher Noble
Norwich, UK — Yuzhen Zhu
Kota Bandung, Indonesia — Fathiro Hutama Reksa Putra

Acknowledgements We have been fortunate enough to interact with many individuals and organisations as part of our research programme—and we have been inspired and encouraged by their dedication to developing quantum technologies for the betterment of society. They have helped to shape our thinking and develop the key issues outlined in this book. We would like to thank the researchers at the Business Model Innovation Research Group, the Institute for Manufacturing (IfM), University of Cambridge, for the stimulating discussions. We thank the following individuals for their help, encouragement, and insights: Dominic O'Brien, Roger McKinlay, Sir Peter Knight, Holly Shaw, Nabil Faradis, Andrew Daley, Mete Atatüre, Andrew Lord, Douglas Paul, Sridhar Tayur, Brian Josephson, Adam Brandenburger, Andrea Ferrari, Tom Newby, Manjari Chandran-Ramesh, Leon Lobo, Thierry Botter, Colm Durkan, Celia Merzbacher, Simone Severini, Caterina Ducati, Adrian Kent, Jonathan Legh-Smith, Marco Paini, Stuart Madnick, Will Oliver, Sir Colin Humphreys and Sir Peter Williams. At the National Quantum Computing Centre, we want to thank Michael Cuthbert, Simon Plant and Rob Whiteman and at the Quantum Software Lab, Elham Kashefi.

A special thanks to Evert Geurtsen for indulging our proposal to conduct research in an uncharted space, and to Sriya Iyer for encouraging our bold idea of writing a book on an emerging topic. We would like to express our thanks and appreciation to Alec Selwyn, our Editor at Palgrave Macmillan, for his guidance and advice. And thank you to Amanda George for so professionally copyediting the drafts of the chapters. We would also like to thank the Economic and Social Research Council (ESRC) via The Productivity Institute, and the Engineering and Physical Sciences Research Council (EPSRC) via the Digital Economy Fellowship, for providing funding for the research. We would further like to acknowledge the EPSRC's longstanding support of quantum technology hubs in the UK, particularly the Quantum Computing & Simulation (QCS) Hub and the Hub for Quantum Computing via Integrated and Interconnected Implementations (QCi3).

Competing Interests The authors have no competing interests to declare that are relevant to the content of this manuscript.

Contents

1	**Introduction**	1
2	**Quantum Computers and Computing a Better World**	33
3	**Quantum Communications and Enhancing Security**	67
4	**Sensing, Imaging, and Timing: Sense, See, and Navigate a Complex World**	95
5	**Summary and Conclusions**	115

Glossary 139

About the Authors

Chander Velu is Professor of Innovation and Economics at the Institute for Manufacturing (IfM), the Department of Engineering, University of Cambridge. He heads the Business Model Innovation Research Group at the IfM. Chander is Fellow at Selwyn College, Cambridge, and Fellow of the Institute of Chartered Accountants in England and Wales. Prior to joining the IfM, Chander was a member of the faculty at Cambridge Judge Business School. He has worked as a consultant with PricewaterhouseCoopers and Booz Allen & Hamilton in London.

Keith Norman is part of the Engagement team in the QCi3 Hub, a collaboration between 18 UK academic institutions and one of five hubs within the UK National Quantum Technologies Programme. He has worked at the University of Cambridge on the business implications of quantum technologies, and was seconded into the Office for Quantum at the UK Department of Science, Innovation and Technology. Keith has over 25 years' experience in industry, and holds a PhD in Particle Physics from the University of Birmingham, based on research he carried out at CERN.

Yuzhen Zhu is a Lecturer/Assistant Professor in Digital Business and Information Systems at Norwich Business School, University of East Anglia (UEA). He holds a PhD in Information Systems Management and his research interest lies in the business and organizational implications of emerging information technologies, particularly on their use, adoption and (eco)systems development. Prior to taking up his current role, he completed his Post-Doc at the University of Cambridge.

Fathiro Hutama Reksa Putra is a lecturer in the Industrial Engineering and Engineering Management Department at Bandung Institute of Technology (ITB). He holds a PhD in Innovation Management from the University of Leeds and a Master's degree in the same field from TU Eindhoven. Fathiro's research interests lie in the intersection between the adoption of emerging technologies, business model innovation, and sustainability transitions. His research has been published in reputable journals such as *Nature* and *Strategic Entrepreneurship Journal*. Prior to joining the ITB, Fathiro was a research associate at the Institute for Manufacturing (IfM), University of Cambridge.

Christopher Noble is Co-Director for Engagement at the QCi3 Hub. He is responsible for the Hub's industrial relations, linking businesses to academia and supporting the UK's growing quantum economy. He is a Chartered Engineer, with a background in advanced manufacturing and emerging technologies. Prior to his role with the QCi3 Hub, Christopher held a variety of engineering and business development positions, and he is a named inventor on several patents.

List of Figures

Fig. 1.1	Length scales	7
Fig. 1.2	Participants at the fifth Solvay Conference in 1927,where much of the groundwork of quantum mechanics was discussed	8
Fig. 1.3	An analogy for quantum superposition	10
Fig. 1.4	The 4Vs business model framework	17
Fig. 1.5	Technology transitions multi-level perspective	19
Fig. 2.1	Moore's law: Number of transistors per microprocessor by year	35
Fig. 2.2	Tiger and money game	40
Fig. 3.1	A simple encoding scheme	69
Fig. 3.2	Quantum key generation example	76
Fig. 5.1	Autonomous vehicles in an envisioned quantum city	119
Fig. 5.2	Industrial emergence framework	121

List of Tables

Table 1.1	Comparison of case studies across macro, meso, and micro levels	25
Table 2.1	Hardware modalities of quantum computers	44
Table 2.2	Potential research questions around quantum computing	62
Table 3.1	Potential research questions around quantum communications	89
Table 4.1	Potential research questions around quantum sensing, imaging, and timing	110

CHAPTER 1

Introduction

This chapter covers:

- *The background to the science of quantum mechanics, and how it has led to interest in business applications;*
- *The UK National Quantum Technologies Programme, other national programmes, and funding;*
- *Some basic principles of quantum mechanics, and why they could lead to economic and societal benefits;*
- *The business and economic issues—Why is it important to study them now?*
- *An analytical framework to help understand the business model innovations;*
- *What key issues need to be explored from a business and economic research perspective?*

Background

Despite the prevalence of digital and related technologies, many societal problems remain challenging. For example, the complexity of understanding atomic interactions and molecular structures makes it challenging to develop new materials to tackle climate change or personalised medicine to treat rare diseases. There is an increasing risk to information security because of the threat of breaking encryption protocols. More

C. Velu et al., *The Business of Quantum Technologies*,
https://doi.org/10.1007/978-3-031-99808-9_1

precise sensing and imaging methods are required for detecting objects below ground level for civil engineering applications, as well as detecting gas leaks in dangerous environments. Moreover, the vulnerability of the global satellite systems calls for more secure and accurate local timing systems. These societal challenges might require quantum technologies to address them.

Over the last 50 years, we have become reliant on certain key technologies that emerged from the quantum mechanics developments of the first half of the twentieth century. The laser, the Magnetic Resonance Imaging (MRI) scanner, and the silicon integrated circuit, which led to digital computers, have collectively become known as part of the "Quantum 1.0 Revolution". In the last decade, we have seen a "Quantum 2.0 Revolution"—a dramatic increase in the promise of quantum technologies to provide benefits to society (GOS, 2016), using a richer set of physical effects, with many nation states increasing funding to quantum research. A dedicated body of international scientists and engineers is working on quantum hardware and algorithms, and new companies have formed to take advantage of this research. Some of these companies are now finding their first customers and beginning to generate revenue (QED-C, 2023).

Given this background, the aim of this book is to address a potential gap between developing these new technologies in academic research centres and industrial settings, and the wider community interested in the interactions between technology and business. It is based on research that the authors have conducted with the wider quantum ecosystem.[1]

The potential applications of these quantum technologies are diverse. The poster child has probably been quantum computing, but there are near-term innovations in communications, security, sensing, imaging, navigation, positioning, and timing. Individually, and combined, these

[1] This included around 65 semi-structured interviews on the subjects of the UK quantum computing landscape, challenges, opportunities, and policy implications. Interviewees came from a range of industries (incumbent firms, quantum start-ups, investors, consulting firms, and system integrators), government sectors (NQCC, UKRI, NQTP) and universities. We held three roundtable discussions on themes of open issues and opportunities in the quantum landscape, and four system integrator events examining business challenges and industrial concerns in quantum computing, skills, and organisational collaboration in the context of quantum technologies. We also participated in several industry panel discussions and training events, academic–industrial meeting days, public dialogue exercises, investor showcases, and other engagement activities with the wider quantum ecosystem. These initiatives and events all contributed to our thinking in writing this book.

technologies have potential applications in finance, healthcare, logistics, defence, computing, and other areas. Some commentators (e.g., Browne et al., 2017) describe these applications as "transformative", possibly to the extent that digital computers, the internal combustion engine, the internet, and television have already transformed society. It is difficult to assess the scale of the future impact, but given the worldwide interest, the rapid progress over the last decade, and the beginnings of several quantum industries, it is plausible that quantum technologies will become general purpose (Bresnahan & Trajtenberg, 1995). However, business managers often encounter a business dilemma and face a challenging trade-off: investing early and being the first mover could provide the foundation to shape and influence the market but comes with risks while waiting till the technology matures might give away the competitive advantage to early adopters (Sodhi & Tayur, 2022). We will explore the putative benefits with transformative impact across multiple application domains in the subsequent chapters.

Government Support and Commercial Investment

Quantum technologies have broad applicability, and several nation states have recognised that quantum technologies are a "good bet" for government support. In parallel, several global commercial organisations (for example, IBM and Google) have made their own strategic investments into quantum technologies, and an ecosystem of new suppliers has started to develop. The balance between government-led support and commercial investment varies. For instance, in China, the majority of quantum technology research is funded by the state. In the USA, commercial organisations have taken more of a lead (McKinsey, 2024).

All of this said, many of the technologies that we will describe in this book are very new, generally still under development, and in many cases, the details of the specific use cases have yet to emerge. Therefore, in addition to funding the basic research, local and national governments also have a role to play in nurturing new industrial players to take technologies from lab to market over an extended timescale.

The UK is a global leader in basic quantum technology research and developing new quantum industries. It was the first country to instantiate a national programme for quantum technologies. The UK National Quantum Technologies Programme was prompted by the 2010 trillion-dollar stock-market crash (the so-called "flash crash"), which was caused by automatic trading algorithms competing with one another and creating instability (Knight, 2019). The proposed solution was to accurately time-stamp transactions using quantum clocks, which led to a planning round that identified the need for four UK quantum technology hubs, plus a quantum metrology institute. The UK Treasury made an initial investment of £270 million to accelerate the development of quantum technologies in quantum imaging, sensing and metrology, and computing and chip-scale encryption. Since 2014, this programme has channelled around £1 billion into developing quantum technology over a 10-year period. Under the programme, the UK quantum technology hubs have evolved into hubs for quantum computing and simulation, quantum communications, quantum imaging, and quantum sensing and timing. A National Quantum Computing Centre has also been launched, which acts as a national laboratory for quantum computing, as well as a related Quantum Software Lab to identify, develop, and validate real-world use cases for quantum computing.

In 2023, the UK government announced its strategic quantum programme for the next 10 years (DSIT, 2023a), which will provide £2.5 billion of funding for a range of quantum initiatives, including five new quantum technology hubs. It also announced the National Quantum Strategy Mission (DSIT, 2023b), with ambitious targets for increased quantum computing power to deliver the next generation of drugs, chemicals, materials and healthcare outcomes, resilient quantum navigation and timing systems for improved accuracy, and more precise quantum sensors to maintain critical infrastructure. These strategic missions are likely to stimulate more research, and crucially they draw more industrial organisations into quantum technology development.[2] Under the national quantum programme, the UK Royal Academy of Engineering

[2] **Mission 1** By 2035, there will be accessible, UK-based quantum computers capable of running 1 trillion operations and supporting applications that provide benefits well in excess of classical supercomputers across key sectors of the economy. **Mission 2** By 2035, the UK will have deployed the world's most advanced quantum network at scale, pioneering the future quantum internet. **Mission 3** By 2030, every NHS Trust will benefit from quantum-sensing-enabled solutions, helping those with chronic illness to live healthier, longer lives through early diagnosis and treatment. **Mission 4** By 2030, quantum navigation systems, including clocks, will be deployed on aircraft, providing next-generation accuracy for resilience that is independent of satellite signals. **Mission 5** By 2030, mobile, networked quantum sensors will have unlocked new situational awareness capabilities, exploited across critical infrastructure in the transport, telecoms, energy, and defence sectors.

has reviewed and made recommendations on the requirements of the UK's quantum infrastructure, including nanofabrication prototyping, packaging, and integration (RAE, 2024).

The quantum programme in the UK has been widely regarded as a success, and many other national and local governments are now investing in quantum technologies, with estimates of global investments at the level of several tens of billion dollars (Qureca, 2023). Countries such as Germany, France, South Korea, and the USA are all broadly investing in quantum technologies at a similar level to the UK, in the order of a few billion pounds, with EU Member States being bolstered by additional funds directly from the EU. Others, for example, Japan, Taiwan, Australia, and Singapore, are investing at the level of hundreds of millions of pounds. China is an outlier, with estimates of quantum investment in the low tens of billion pounds, representing a substantial proportion of total global investment (McKinsey, 2024).

What Is Quantum?

This section briefly introduces quantum science. There are many more complete texts on the subject (e.g., Levin, 2002), but we aim to give the reader enough of a quantum mechanics background that they can understand and appreciate how quantum technologies work.

Let us begin with a thought experiment. Imagine climbing a hill. For the sake of argument, let us assume the slope of the hill is a constant, so in the thought experiment, imagine walking up a smoothly tarmacked road with no bumps. Climbing the hill will take some energy. We can choose how much energy to use with every step. A big step will take more energy than a small step, and we can choose how big our steps are, depending on the length of our legs. In our thought experiment, we can imagine our legs being as long as we like, so in principle we can take steps of any length, as long as we have enough energy. Correspondingly, the amount of energy we expend with each step can take any value, arbitrarily large or small.

This principle that energy can take any value was widely accepted by scientists at the end of the nineteenth century. They had become used to applying the principle of energy to a range of scientific and engineering problems, based on the assumption that energy could take any value and vary smoothly between those values.

However, there was a problem with this view. At the end of the nineteenth century, scientists' best predictions were unable to explain the colour of light emitted as the temperature of an object increased. Consider a piece of metal heated by a fire – as the temperature increases, the metal glows dull orange, then yellow, and ultimately white hot. However, increasing the temperature further has little impact on the frequency or intensity of the emitted light. The existing theory at the time predicted that the total power radiated should grow without limit at ultraviolet frequencies and higher. Classical 19th-century physics assumed that oscillators within the object could vibrate at any frequency, absorbing or emitting energy continuously. In this model, oscillators with higher frequencies (shorter wavelengths, falling into the ultraviolet range) could hold increasingly large amounts of energy. The theory predicted that, as the temperature increased, these high-frequency oscillators would become increasingly energetic, leading to the object radiating a disproportionate amount of energy in the ultraviolet spectrum, ultimately reaching infinity. This became something of an embarrassment to the scientific community—in later years, physicist Paul Ehrenfest effectively coined the term "ultraviolet catastrophe" to describe the failure of the theory (Ehrenfest, 1911).

Then, at the turn of the century, an idea emerged that appeared to resolve the issue. Instead of assuming that the energy absorbed and emitted by an object as it was heated up could take any value, Max Planck proposed that energy comes in packets of a fixed, tiny size (Planck, 1901), and this idea was later elaborated by Einstein (1905). This is the origin of the use of the Latin word "*quantum*", in the sense of *how much* energy is in each packet. These quanta are proportional to the frequency of the radiation, where the oscillators can only exist at specific energy levels. Planck's original proposition was that the quanta were merely a mathematical trick, but Einstein later showed they were real physical objects, with measurable characteristics.

To return to our thought experiment, imagine that instead of climbing a hill on a smooth pathway, we are climbing a set of stairs. We are no longer free to take any step length we choose. If we are to have our feet on a stair, we can only choose step lengths that match the stair height. We could choose to climb two or three stairs at a time, but we cannot take steps of half a stair height, or two-thirds of a stair height – our step length must match a whole number of stairs. The energy we need our legs to provide must therefore increase stepwise. Planck proposed that these similar stepwise jumps in energy were what was happening when heating objects and measuring the colours of light emitted, albeit at minuscule scales. With quantisation, oscillators can only absorb or emit a whole number of quanta corresponding to their specific frequency. This limits how much energy a high-frequency oscillator can hold, with a reduced probability of reaching very high energy states, and hence a reduction in the intensity of ultraviolet and higher-frequency light.

This proposition marked the beginning of a new field of science, quantum physics, describing the rules of nature obeyed by objects at the scale of atoms and smaller. Bearing in mind that all matter that we interact with is made of atoms, ultimately quantum physics describes the behaviour of all matter. However, many of the effects of quantum physics are only observable at roughly the size scale of atoms and smaller. This means that quantum effects generally become important at scales of around one-millionth of a millimetre. Although tiny, these scales cover many phenomena, some of which are shown in Fig. 1.1.

These scales where quantum effects dominate are much smaller than can be observed by eye, or even microscope, so they were not well understood by scientists until the early decades of the twentieth century. From

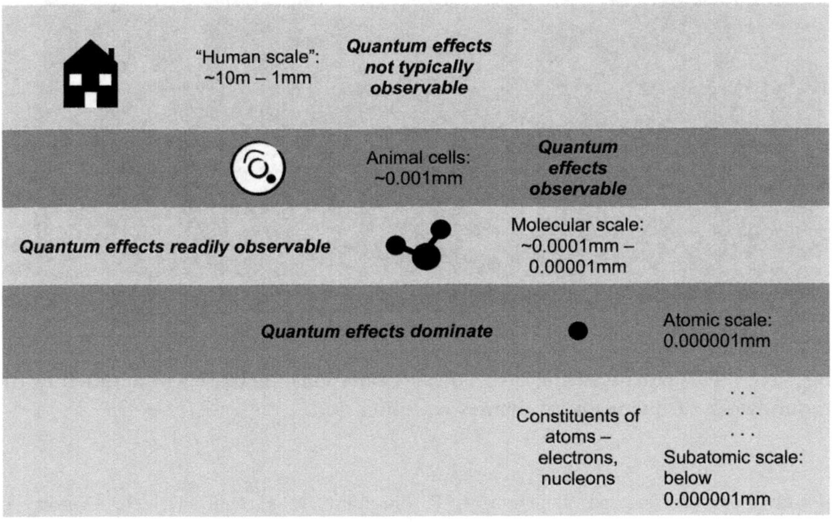

Fig. 1.1 Length scales

around 1900–30, there was a revolution in the understanding of nature at these length scales, and quantum mechanics emerged as a new branch of science to explain how nature works at these small sizes. Following Planck's proposal that energy was quantised, Werner Heisenberg and Erwin Schrödinger independently developed mathematical frameworks to explain the spectrum of energy emitted by atoms (Heisenberg, 1925; Schrödinger, 1926). These frameworks looked very different but were ultimately shown by Paul Dirac and others to be consistent with one another (Dirac, 1927). By the time the fifth Solvay Conference took place in 1927 (Fig. 1.2), much of the theoretical groundwork had been completed.

Fig. 1.2 Participants at the fifth Solvay Conference in 1927,where much of the groundwork of quantum mechanics was discussed[3]

[3] *Back row*: A. Piccard, E. Henriot, P. Ehrenfest, E. Herzen, Th. De Donder, E. Schrödinger, J. E. Verschaffelt, W. Pauli, W. Heisenberg, R. H. Fowler, L. Brillouin; *Middle row*: P. Debye, M. Knudsen, W. L. Bragg, H. A. Kramers, P. A. M. Dirac, A. H. Compton, L. de Broglie, M. Born, N. Bohr; *Front row*: I. Langmuir, M. Planck, M.

This science has developed over the last 100 years, and the basic results are now very well accepted as mainstream science, supported by a vast amount of experimental evidence. It applies at the scale of atoms, and the constituent parts of atoms (electrons, atomic nuclei, and their constituents), and describes the interactions between objects at this scale. Experimental evidence has confirmed the predictions of quantum theory to astonishing levels of accuracy, at around one part in one trillion, equivalent to being able to predict the diameter of the Sun to an accuracy of the width of a human hair.

The principles of quantum physics that apply to our discussion about quantum technologies are not difficult to understand, even though interpreting these principles has been the subject of debate for many years. Two of the most important principles relevant to our discussion of quantum technologies are *the superposition of quantum states* and *entanglement*. In subsequent chapters, we will explore some other quantum principles, such as Heisenberg's uncertainty principle, but since superposition and entanglement underpin most of the technologies that are part of the Quantum 2.0 Revolution, we will describe these in more detail below.

Quantum States and Superposition

Quantum mechanical objects (atoms, sub-atomic particles, etc.) have a *state* – a number or series of numbers that describe that object mathematically. Depending on the mathematical representation, the state describes the energy of that object, or other properties, but, regardless of the representation, it is a description of that object in mathematical terms. As an analogy, let us consider a coin. Coins are not quantum mechanical objects in the way atoms are, but they do have a state—heads or tails.

Quantum mechanical states are not generally well-defined values. Again, as an analogy, if we flip a coin, then while it is spinning in the air, for all practical purposes, it is neither heads nor tails but a *combination of both states*. Similarly, quantum mechanical objects tend to exist in combinations of states. What happens when we measure the state of a quantum mechanical object? In our coin analogy, the measurement is made when we grab the spinning coin out of the air. At that point, we

Curie, H. A. Lorentz, A. Einstein, P. Langevin, Ch. E. Guye, C. T. R. Wilson, O. W. Richardson.

never find the coin to be in a combination of heads and tails—we only ever observe *either* heads *or* tails. Similarly, when a quantum mechanical state is measured, the only outcome ever observed ***is a well-defined value for that state***.

The coin analogy is not perfect, but for our purposes, it is close enough to the behaviour of objects around the scale of atoms or smaller. The concept of the quantum mechanical state can be more rigorously defined, and atoms are "more quantum" than our coin analogy, but this does not concern us in this context.

To restate, atoms and objects of similar size have *states*, much as coins have heads and tails states. In general, these states are ***combinations of all allowed states*** (like a spinning coin being a combination of heads and tails) ***until they are measured*** (like a flipped coin when it is caught). When measured, the combination of states is never observed—we always see one definite state. In the coin analogy, we always observe heads or tails when we catch the coin—never a combination of the two (see Fig. 1.3).

The technical term for this principle of quantum objects being in multiple states at the same time is ***superposition***. Most objects at a human scale do not measurably obey the principle of superposition—things are generally in one state or another, but never both states at the same time. However, some things at human scale do at least have analogues of superposition, for example spinning coins (i.e., a combination of heads and tails), rolling dice (a combination of 1–6), or spinning roulette wheels (a combination of 0–36). These analogies also capture the idea of "dropping into" one state when measured—coins are either heads or tails when caught, dice land with a side uppermost rather than on their edges, and roulette wheels stop on a definite number.

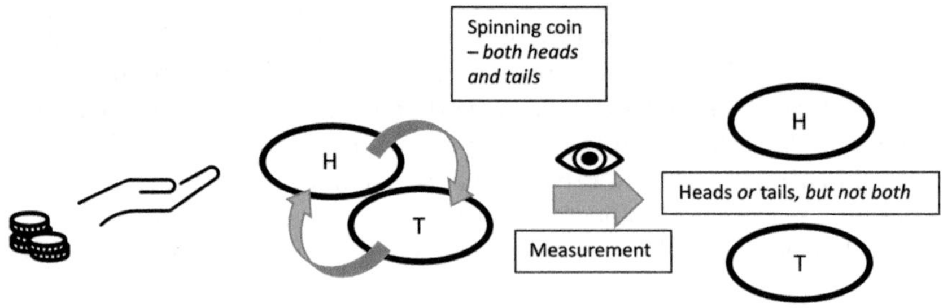

Fig. 1.3 An analogy for quantum superposition

Quantum Entanglement

Our spinning coins also lead to a discussion about a second important principle of quantum mechanics that is very relevant to the technologies being considered. Imagine we each toss a coin in the air. While the coins are spinning in the air, they are individually in a combination of their own heads and tails states—they are in individual superpositions of heads and tails. Imagine we both grab our respective coins out of the air and catch them on the back of our hands. You look at your coin—let us say you see heads. Without seeing my coin, what can you say about whether my coin is heads or tails? The correct answer is "nothing". The two coins are independent, so what happened to your coin has no impact on mine. By looking at your coin, you have gained no information about my coin. On that basis you certainly should not choose to bet on the outcome of my coin toss based on the outcome of yours. If you observed that when you get heads I am also more likely to get heads, you should realise something is amiss.

However, our two-coin analogy does not hold for quantum objects. Physicists can prepare two quantum mechanical objects (again, we emphasise this means two atoms, or something of similar scale or smaller) in such a way that *both* objects are described by *just one* quantum state. Take a moment to consider this: it is not that both objects are described by identical quantum states; the two objects are no longer independent and can only be described by a single quantum state shared between them. If I now give you one of these quantum objects and you make a measurement on it, the second object in the pair remains correlated to the first. In our coin analogy, this is like preparing two coins in a certain mysterious way and then taking one coin each. We both toss our respective coins. Let us say you get tails. I grab my coin from the air just after you grab yours. Because of how I have prepared them, our coins remain correlated, and there is now an increased probability that I too will get tails. We emphasise this is *not* how normal coins behave. If you were betting on the outcome of my coin tosses and found that whenever you get tails there is an increased probability I will get tails, you would again think something were amiss, and you would want to know what I had done to prepare the coins in this way. In reality, there is no way to prepare coins like this.

However, quantum mechanical objects can be prepared in this state. The technical term for this preparation is called *entanglement*. Most of the electrons in the atoms in your body naturally find themselves in this entangled state: they do not even need an external agent to prepare them; their natural configuration in an atom forces them into an entangled state with other electrons (Briegel & Popescu, 2014). The quantum state of each of these electrons can only be defined in relation to other entangled electrons—they cannot be described as independent entities. Knowing the state of one entangled electron immediately gives us information about the other electrons with which it is entangled.

This may sound obscure, but entanglement is the defining property of quantum mechanics (Schrödinger, 1935). Coins, dice, and roulette wheels all display analogues of superposition, but only atoms and objects at a similar scale display the property of entanglement—this is part of the reason why the properties of coins, dice and roulette wheels can only provide analogies for quantum mechanics. Understanding, in broad terms, the principles of superposition and entanglement provides the background to understanding all quantum technologies.

Summary of Quantum Mechanics

At this point, we provide a summary of the key points below:

1. *Quantum mechanics is the science of the very small, at the scale of atoms and smaller. Typical quantum mechanical objects (i.e., things that obey the rules of quantum mechanics) are therefore atoms and their constituents (electrons, atomic nuclei,* etc.*), particles of light (photons), and so on. The science of quantum mechanics has developed over the last hundred years or so and is now well understood.*
2. *Quantum mechanical objects are described by quantum states, which, for many cases relevant to a quantum technology context, can be thought of in terms of the analogy to the states of a coin (heads or tails).*
3. *Quantum states are generally described by a superposition of all possible quantum states that object can take. In the coin analogy, this is like the general state of a spinning coin—it is neither heads nor tails but a combination of the two.*
4. *When we measure a quantum state, we never find it in a superposition. We only ever observe it to be in one definite quantum state. In the coin analogy, this is like catching the spinning coin—we only ever observe it to be heads or tails, never a superposition of both.*

5. *Quantum states can become entangled. This means that multiple quantum objects are described by a single quantum state, and there is no way to describe them as individual quantum objects when they are maximally entangled. This would be like flipping more than one coin at the same time and observing that when the coins are caught they all land heads or all tails. Coins do not behave in this way, but it is very common for quantum mechanical objects to be in this entangled state.*

Superposition and entanglement are fundamental quantum properties. Although we have described them using macroscopic, classical analogues (e.g., spinning coins), in subsequent chapters, we will discuss how these quantum properties allow new ways of storing and manipulating information that are not possible classically. This opens the door to a range of new technologies, including quantum computing, communications, sensing, imaging, and timing. Developing these technologies will require new business models to allow these technologies to diffuse more broadly. We now look at the business and economic implications.

Business and Economic Issues

Let us begin with a simple question: Why is it important to study the business and economic issues of quantum technologies now? If the science of quantum mechanics has existed for more than a hundred years, what has changed recently to mean there are business issues to discuss? There are several answers to this question. First, the 2010s saw rapid growth in global investment in quantum technologies, partly driven by the developments in the 1990s, which showed that quantum computers might significantly speed up some computations and possibly break existing information encryption protocols. Things that had only been ideas 10 or 20 years before were receiving research funding, either state-sponsored (e.g., the UK national programme) or industrially sponsored (e.g., Google and IBM investing in quantum computing). By the early 2020s, this has led to an increase in the number of firms with technology that is ready to exploit, or likely to be ready to exploit in the relatively short term. Second, observing this investment, many large industrial organisations have started to investigate quantum technologies in their own settings, leading to an increase in potential industrial use cases of quantum technologies. Third, although it is not possible to predict which quantum technologies will become dominant, a window of opportunity is now opening to explore these issues as a "living laboratory".

We will consider the evolution of a technological life cycle, followed by a business and economic perspective on such technological change. We will use the business model as a lens to assess the business and economic perspectives.

The evolution of a technology in industry usually undergoes a relatively extended period of incremental change with the emergence of a dominant design, which is punctuated by technological discontinuities (Anderson & Tushman, 1990; Tushman & Anderson, 1986). Specifically, existing technologies could be significantly influenced by new foci technologies, which opens up an era where multiple variations of the foci technology can exist until a dominant design is reached. The dominant design of the foci technology could yield an incremental change and steady improvement of the foci technology, which could be disrupted by another new technology, contributing to "technological discontinuity". Some studies have emphasised that incumbent firms often focus on improving the performance of existing technologies based on customer requirements (Christensen, 1997; Christensen & Bower, 1996). This emphasis on improving the performance of existing technologies can lead to incumbent firms losing their leading positions in their industry, as entrants adopt new technologies to serve the needs of niche customers, and these new technologies eventually become the dominant design. For example, we have witnessed the emergence of new firms that become the leading firm in each new technology in the data storage industry (from magnetic tape to hard disk, and floppy disk to flash drive, respectively).

Utterback and his colleagues' work (1975, 1993, 1996) further suggests that such technological evolution emerges and develops as firms interact with their environment. From Utterback's perspective, technologies evolve across three stages: in the first *fluid stage* the foci technology remains largely unknown for its potential performance, and the market and supply chain gradually become less stable, leading to wide interactions between the firm and its environment to resolve the technological and economic uncertainties. As these interactions unfold and accumulate, the foci technology evolves and enters the second, *transitional stage*, where the component supply chain and market demand become stabilised and the dominant design emerges. The emergence of a product's dominant design shifts the emphasis of the technology from product innovation to process innovation (the third, *specific stage*). In particular, as the dominant design benchmarks against various performance criteria and incrementally improves product architecture, the foci technology evolves to a stage where greater emphasis is put on process innovation. This continues until another new technology is introduced, potentially with substantially different and substitutive technological or economic benefits, leading to a discontinuity of the foci technology in the industry, and a new technology or technological innovation cycle between firms and their environment begins from the fluid stage. The technological evolution is highly connected with firms' business activities, among which firms' business models play a central role. The business model is thus critical to understanding the business and economics of a foci technology or technological innovation.

Given this background, adopting quantum technologies could result in a reduction in productivity growth before the economic benefits accrue fully because of the "steep learning curve" that industries might face adapting to the technology and developing new business models (Velu & Putra, 2023). Moreover, the benefits of quantum technologies need to reach all parts of society in a responsible way (Ten Holter et al., 2021). To ease the learning curve and ensure that the benefits of quantum technologies accrue fairly to society, we need to better understand the barriers and enablers to building an appropriate business ecosystem in order to scale up the technology and spur economic growth.

Business Models

A business model can be conceptualised as a complex organisational system that transforms inputs into outputs in terms of valuable propositions for customers (Velu, 2024). Business models often act as the arc that connects technology with the ability to deliver a compelling customer value proposition. The capability to adopt new technologies, and develop associated business models, is potentially a major source of productivity gains and growth for new and incumbent firms (OECD, 2015). Business models can be seen as a form of activity system that connects the internal features of the firm, such as resources and routines, with the external aspects, such as partners, markets, and customers, thus defining how the firm goes to market to implement the strategy (Baden-Fuller & Haefliger, 2013; Zott & Amit, 2010; Zott et al., 2011). The business model as an activity system has three key design parameters: *content, structure,* and *governance* (Zott & Amit, 2010). *Content* describes which activities are considered to be part of the business model. *Structure* is about how these activities are connected to one another. Finally, *governance* relates to how—and to whom—the responsibilities are given to make decisions about them. The business model acts as a mechanism for managers to collectively form a common understanding based on rules, norms, and beliefs in order to guide their choices (Chesbrough & Rosenbloom, 2002; Doganova & Eyquem-Renault, 2009). In this sense, business models are the "architecture" that provides the overarching connection between the value created for customers and the value captured by the business in terms of profit.[4]

Components of the Business Model

A business model is a complex system with components that link (1) the customer value proposition, (2) how value is created, (3) the means of value capture, and (4) the partners in the value network (Velu, 2017, 2024). We propose that these elements are the "4Vs" of the business model: value proposition, value creation, value capture, and value network (Velu, 2018). Specifically:

1. **Value proposition** refers to how the firm defines and communicates the benefits for its stakeholders, such as customers, in a unique and compelling way.
2. **Value creation** refers to the process through which the firm generates value for its stakeholders within the business, which usually includes technology design, R&D and production, storage and distribution activities, and after-sales services.
3. **Value capture** demonstrates the means through which the firm captures and converts the created value into the firm's revenue or profits, which defines the revenue and cost architectures and the associated financing structures.
4. **Value network** describes the ecosystem of partners that the firm needs to develop its business value.

This is illustrated in Fig. 1.4.

[4] This includes a holistic perspective covering value for all stakeholders.

Fig. 1.4 The 4Vs business model framework (adapted from Velu, 2018)

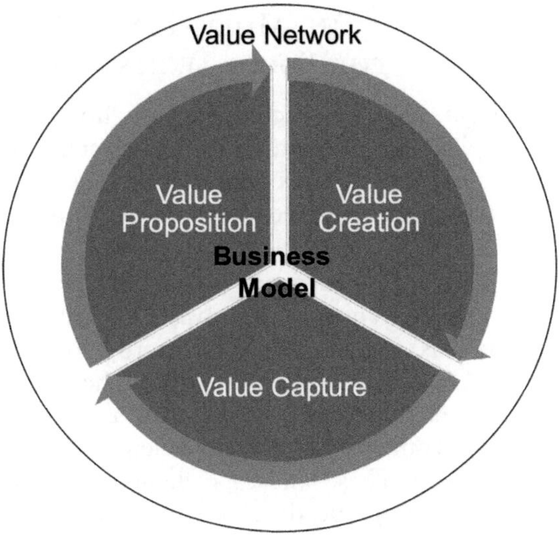

The 4Vs business model framework encapsulates the economic aspects of how value is created, delivered to the customer and other stakeholders, and captured by the firm. A complementary framework is the cognitive perspective on how business models shape managerial choices (Baden-Fuller & Mangematin, 2013). The cognitive perspective articulates how senior management frames the business model, and how it can influence their decisions and actions in order to create and capture value.

Business model innovation articulates the discovery and adoption of fundamentally different modes of value proposition, value creation and/or capture, and the value network from an existing business. Business model innovation redefines an existing product or service, and how it is provided to customers and stakeholders, by identifying unique configurations of business model components (Velu & Jacob, 2016). Business model innovation often takes place within an industrial system where social and technical aspects need to be jointly considered.

The Multi-Level Perspective for Socio-Technical Transition

The multi-level perspective explains how technology-enabled transition takes place in a multi-connected system in an evolutionary process over time. It identifies three levels—landscape, regime, and niche—to understand changes in consumption–production systems (Geels, 2002):

1. The *landscape* demonstrates the contextual change at the macro level of transition. It consists of elements such as political ideology, beliefs, structures, and macro-economic change, and it usually evolves slowly (Geels, 2012). The landscape level consists of deep structural trends, social values, and worldviews, largely beyond the control of the system actors, for example policies on climate change. These landscape elements put pressure on other levels, such as guiding the development orientation for regimes and creating windows of opportunity for niches.
2. The *regime* refers to a meso-level socio-technical system, composed of multiple interconnected elements such as science, market, customers, industry, policy, technology, and culture (Fuenfschilling & Binz, 2018; Geels, 2002). These elements are interrelated and engage in a co-evolutionary development, where change in one element could lead to change in others. The regime is steadily developed under the pressure of the landscape and, in turn, reinforces the evolution of the landscape. Thanks to the windows created by the landscape, the regime could be changed by rapid innovations from niches, leading to restructuring or reconfiguration, with a systemic change (Geels, 2014).
3. *Niches* describe the micro-level change and are usually rapid. Niches are often spaces where novel technological practices emerge and are nurtured, comprising innovative activities such as experimentation, piloting, technology design, and learning during technology development (Rip & Kemp, 1998). Niche-level efforts can reinforce and be protected by regime and landscape efforts, but they can also alter regimes when windows of opportunity are created by the landscape, eventually leading to rapid change in the socio-technical regime (Geels, 2002).

Technology transition frameworks based on the multi-level perspective tend to differentiate between four different phases of transition, namely, experimentation (phase 1), stabilisation (phase 2), diffusion (phase 3), and institutionalisation (phase 4) (Geels, 2019, pp. 190–92). Phase 1 consists of firms experimenting and learning from various trials being conducted. Phase 2 consists of innovations gaining traction, and the clarity of consolidation in a defined direction. Phase 3 consists of adoption in mainstream markets. Phase 4 consists of replacing the components of the previous consumption-production system, including certain accepted norms, habits, institutional arrangements, and standards. The summary framework is shown in Fig. 1.5.

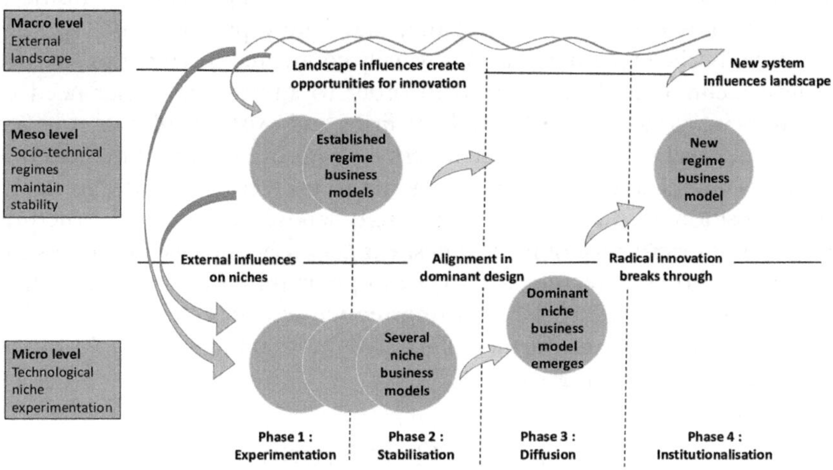

Fig. 1.5 Technology transitions multi-level perspective Adapted from: Geels, F. W. (2002). Technological transitions as evolutionary reconfiguration processes: a multi-level perspective and a case-study. Research Policy, 31(8–9), 1257–1274; Geels, F. W. (2019). Socio-technical transitions to sustainability: a review of criticisms and elaborations of the multi-level perspective. Current Opinion in Environmental Sustainability, 39, 187–201; Velu, C., & Putra, F. H. (2023). How to introduce quantum computers without slowing economic growth. Nature, 619(7970), 461–464

An Integrated Framework of Technology Transition and Business Models

Given the right landscape conditions, radical niche innovations can overthrow dominant regimes and enable transition pathways for new technologies (Geels & Schot, 2007). The focus of the multi-level perspective is the evolutionary mechanism of change, with less explicit recognition of the agency and politics of change. Business models provide the agency for such change, and they play a central role at the micro and meso levels of socio-technical transition (Velu, 2024). New technologies often require the creation of new markets with an initial business model before scaling up and pivoting the business model to develop commercially viable propositions (Velu, 2024). New technology-enabled transitions thus occur when the niche, regime, and landscape levels interact and coalesce. Niche experimentation is usually conducted by start-ups to drive radical technological innovations in order to address an unmet need or create new market needs. Incumbent firms and existing rules or routines at regime level steadily and instrumentally improve existing practices and business model activities, initially tending to protect the status quo unless their position is threatened. The macro landscape, such as structural trends and macro-economic changes, exogenously impacts and forces the transition process, creating windows of opportunity for niche innovation to break through and replace existing regime activities.

These forces can be further illustrated by examining some historical cases of technological transitions.

Business Case Studies

UK Transition to Sustainable Energy

The transition to a sustainable energy supply network shows that the business model design needs to be incorporated within technology transition systems. The landscape-level changes due to the sustainable energy transition provide the context for better understanding the importance of business model design across the multi-level perspective model.

The transition to combined power and heat (CHP) systems with district-level localised heating in the UK enabled multiple approaches that incentivised start-ups or incumbent firms, respectively (Bolton & Hannon, 2016):

- In the niche-based start-up approach (the niche in the multi-level perspective), the local authority owns part of a start-up energy service firm and promotes the council's sustainability objectives. The start-up energy service firm might compete with incumbents to provide energy services based on decentralised energy solutions.
- The incumbent-based model consists of the local authority contracting to buy energy services from third-party incumbent energy firms. The local authority provides the anchor loads, such as large municipal buildings and residential schemes, as the principal customer. The local authority enters into a long-term contract with the incumbent energy service provider to encourage the large capital investment needed for the local CHP schemes. This tends to maintain the meso-level dynamics.

These two models might be driven by different socio-political considerations, for example whether a local authority should own an energy service firm. In addition, the transition could be driven by a start-up or an incumbent firm. Moreover, the two models of transition to a sustainable energy supply framework show that the business model design needs to be incorporated within the technology transition systems.

US Transition to Solar Energy

The transition from one technology to another often takes place in a non-linear path that might entail periods of failure and fairly settled development, followed by rapid acceleration (Hess, 2023). Moreover, the process of change is multi-causal, with different forces acting on the change process simultaneously, exerting varying influences. Hess (2023) analyses the development of distributed solar energy (DSE) in the USA over five decades from the 1970s, focusing on the political conflicts and tensions between niche firms working on a coalition promoting solar photovoltaic technologies, and incumbent firms tied to coal and nuclear power. During the 1970s in the USA, the increasing use of air-conditioning and urban demand resulted in electricity burn-outs and a shortage of heating oil. Moreover, in the early 1970s the Organization of the Petroleum Exporting Countries (OPEC) launched an oil embargo on countries that supported Israel during the Yum Kippur war, including the USA. In addition, there was an increasing movement to oppose the use of nuclear energy, which gained momentum with the partial nuclear meltdown at Three Mile Island in Pennsylvania. The combination of these factors led to a reconsideration of energy security. Hence, solar energy became part of the mix of proposals for a new national energy policy. The solar advocates were divided between the large utility-scale solar by incumbent firms and entrepreneurial DSE start-ups.

During the late 1970s, the US administration was led by President Jimmy Carter, a Democrat who was supportive of emerging renewable energy technologies such as DSE. Carter had implemented a variety of tax credit and government support through bloc-buy programmes. The incumbent firms' base energy load came from coal and nuclear energy. Hence, they opposed the development of niche solar start-up firms unless they were compatible with the incumbent's strategy of maintaining coal and nuclear energy sources and only using solar as a backup for the load.

During the Republican government of Ronald Reagan in the 1980s, the Administration cut subsidies and taxes to the emerging solar industry. The early 1990s brought landscape changes that reopened opportunities that had closed under the Reagan administration. In particular, the invasion of Kuwait and the Gulf War of the 1990s increased national concerns about energy security from oil—hence, there was renewed interest in solar.

Moreover, during the 1990s, the publication of reports by the Inter-Governmental Panel on Climate Change and the negotiation of the Kyoto Protocol agreement started global landscape changes, with increased momentum for long-term energy transition. Although the US Congress failed to ratify the Kyoto Protocol, there was growing support for renewable energy initiatives from 1993 to 2000, under the governance of Democrat President Bill Clinton.

Under President George Bush, who was elected in 2000, planning for energy transition was transferred from federal to state governance. The states introduced net metering, allowing energy to be sold back to the grid at favourable retail prices, which encouraged the development of DSE. Although the incumbent firms were still adopting tactics to discourage net metering, the solar industry found support among the anti-nuclear movement and climate-change organisations during the 2000s, which helped to build momentum for DSE.

By the early 2010s, the costs of solar energy had started to reduce because of technology innovation, and cheaper products from Asian suppliers increased demand. A more fundamental change is now occurring: enabling small-scale photo photovoltaics, battery storage, and other distributed energy resources to integrate into the existing system configuration is stimulating changes at the industrial level for energy production and distribution.

Norwegian Transition to Electric Vehicles

The emergence and diffusion of electric vehicles (EVs) in Norway offer valuable insights into the process of technology transition from internal combustion engines to electricity-driven vehicles (Ryghaug & Skjølsvold, 2023). The oil crisis of 1973 prompted Norway, a major oil producer, to think about alternative energy sources for vehicles. Owing to Norway's geographical setting, hydropower was a key energy source. The combination of government policy to subsidise electric vehicles, and building the electric charging system, enabled Norway to move rapidly to an EV model. This had two effects. The first effect was the emergence of a pro-environmental attitude by the Norwegian population following the adoption of EV, which had a spillover effect into behavioural characteristics such as an increase in solar-panel installations at the homes of EV vehicle owners. Second, the success of EV adoption in Norway has increased the electrification of buses, ferries, and heating and port systems. The increasing use of electricity for transportation also encouraged the building of battery factories along the coast.

US Bond Trading Market Transition to Digital Technologies

Opposition by incumbent firms was also evident in the US bond trading market following the advent of the internet in the early 2000s (Velu, 2016). The conventional approach to trading bonds is for banks to act as an intermediary market maker for investor firms such as asset-management firms. A plethora of new entrants launched electronic trading platforms to disintermediate existing incumbent banks by enabling direct trading between investors of securities. The dominant incumbent banks were reluctant to change their business models, but the less dominant ones were willing to adopt incremental business model innovations. These innovations were compatible with the existing business practices of acting as an intermediary, but they made the process more efficient by adopting internet-based trading protocols. This was because the less dominant incumbent banks initially had more to lose from the emergence of new entrants, as they held less market share. Therefore, losing a few customers could affect their profitability more than it could the dominant banks. However, as the start-up firms and less dominant banks adopted the innovation afforded by the internet, this affected the customer base of the dominant banks. Hence, when the dominant banks' profitability was threatened over time, they decided to adopt revolutionary business models—in some cases buying some of the incumbent firms to try to integrate their niche business models into their core business.

Table 1.1 summarises the case studies discussed above through the lens of the multi-level perspective. This allows us to gain an overarching view of how business models develop given technological change, and it helps us to think about the patterns in that development. These patterns may be useful in thinking about how business models will need to adapt in light of quantum technologies, and how these business models could accelerate quantum technology adoption.

Summary of Case Studies

Table 1.1 Comparison of case studies across macro, meso, and micro levels

	UK Transition to Sustainable Energy	*US Transition to Solar*	*Norwegian Transition to EV*	*US Bond Trading Transition*
Macro level—external landscape	Transition to sustainable energy supply network: district-level combined heat and power systems	Government cuts subsidies for renewables. Kuwait and Gulf Wars, and Kyoto Protocol raise concerns about supply. Transfer to state-level solar energy cost reductions	The 1973 oil crisis prompts thinking about alternative energy. EV subsidies and scale-up of electric charging system	Rise of the internet enables new trading models
Meso level—existing regimes	Incumbent energy firms contracted by local authorities, which supply anchor loads (large municipal buildings, etc.)	Incumbents oppose state net metering. Some niche players become incumbent suppliers	Existing transport authorities invest in electrification (e.g., buses), leading to battery factories along coast	Dominant incumbents maintain status quo. Less dominant firms adopt innovation. Eventually, dominant incumbents start to buy niche firms
Micro level—niche players	Local authority buys stake in start-up(s) and promotes sustainability objectives. Start-ups compete to provide CHP to local authority	Net metering encourages the development of solar, plus other support. Cheaper products from Asia increase demand	Increase in pro-environmental attitudes	New electronic trading platforms that enable direct trading

Conclusion

In summary, these interactions across niche, regime, and landscape levels enable the adoption of new technologies and associated business model innovations. Combining the multi-level perspective and the business model framework highlights several salient features. First, the design of the business model is a key driver of the incentives for firms to adopt and transform how value is created and captured. Second, incumbent firms tend to, at least initially, resist any substantial changes to the approach to the industrial architecture, only engaging with new start-up firms that will enhance, rather than disrupt, their position. Third, new firms need to work with incumbent firms to enhance their position in the marketplace or, alternatively, develop radically different value propositions that could disrupt the market. Fourth, external landscape developments such as social trends and political policies can significantly impact how alignment occurs across the meso levels with incumbent firms, and micro levels with new firms, influencing the technology transition trajectory across the maturity ladder. Fifth, the adoption of new technologies often gives rise to learning and changes in cognitive, social, and business attitudes, which could result in new value propositions, reconfiguration of business models, and spill-over to related areas of technology adoption. Hence, the emergence of new technologies calls for the initial business model to play the role of a market creation or market shaping device, as a pathway to reinventing the business model in order to contribute to financial and economic returns (Velu, 2024). An illustrative example of this approach is when the American Telephone and Telegraph Company (AT&T) built the long-distance telephone service in the early part of the twentieth century in the USA. The initial objective was not commercial, but rather to consolidate the independent Bell companies and help build a public-relations campaign to legitimise the value of long-distance calls for the American people—hence, the long-distance call business was not profitable initially and only made viable economic returns much later (MacDougall, 2006).

In the subsequent chapters, we will explore how the multi-level perspective applies to emerging quantum technologies, and where the macro, meso, and micro levels of development will have an impact. Through case vignettes, we will examine how incentive structures, incumbents' strategic posturing between a pro-active stance and resistance, the interplay of new entrants partnering with incumbents, the degree of radical innovation, social and political forces, and learning and cognitive aspects are likely to play a role in the transition towards a quantum-enabled economy.

Key Points from This Chapter

- A range of diverse technologies are being developed that rely on the practical implementations of quantum mechanical phenomena.
- Quantum mechanics is the science of the very small, applying at the scale of atoms and sub-atomic particles. It has been studied for more than a hundred years and is now mainstream science.
- Quantum mechanical objects have a *state*, although the state is generally not well defined until it is measured. This lack of definition is referred to as *superposition*. Multiple quantum mechanical objects can be (and often are) in a special state where they lose their unique state descriptions; they are described by a single state shared between all of the objects. This property is called *entanglement* and is important in many quantum technologies.
- As these technologies emerge, it will be important to consider the implications for business models. We have proposed the "4Vs" to define business models: value proposition, value creation, value capture, and value network.
- The multi-level perspective explains how technology-enabled transition takes place in a multi-connected system in an evolutionary process over time. It identifies three levels—landscape, regime, and niche—to understand changes in consumption–production systems.

References

Anderson, P., & Tushman, M. L. (1990). Technological discontinuities and dominant designs: A cyclical model of technological change. *Administrative Science Quarterly, 35*, 604–633.

Baden-Fuller, C., & Haefliger, S. (2013). Business models and technological innovation. *Long Range Planning, 46*(6), 419–426.

Baden-Fuller, C., & Mangematin, V. (2013). Business models: A challenging agenda. *Strategic Organization, 11*(4), 418–427.

Bolton, R., & Hannon, M. (2016). Governing sustainability transitions through business model innovation: Towards a systems understanding. *Research Policy, 45*(9), 1731–1742.

Bresnahan, T. F., & Trajtenberg, M. (1995). General purpose technologies "Engines of growth"? *Journal of Econometrics, Elsevier, 65*(1), 83–108.

Briegel, H. J., & Popescu, S. (2014). *Quantum effects in Biology*. Cambridge University Press.

Browne, D., Bose, S., Mintert, F., & Kim, M. (2017). From quantum optics to quantum technologies. *Progress in Quantum Electronics, 54*, 2–18.

Chesbrough, H., & Rosenbloom, R. S. (2002). The role of the business model in capturing value from innovation: Evidence from Xerox Corporation's technology spin-off companies. *Industrial and Corporate Change, 11*(3), 529–555.

Christensen, C. M. (1997). *The innovator's Dilemma*. Harvard Business School Press.

Christensen, C. M., & Bower, J. L. (1996). Customer power, strategic investment, and the failure of leading firms. *Strategic Management Journal, 17*(3), 197–218.

Dirac, P. (1927). The physical interpretation of the quantum dynamics. *Proceedings of the Royal Society A, 113*(765), 621–641.

Doganova, L., & Eyquem-Renault, M. (2009). What do business models do? Innovation devices in technology entrepreneurship. *Research Policy, 38*(10), 1559–1570.

DSIT (Department for Science, Innovation and Technology). (2023a). *National quantum strategy*. https://assets.publishing.service.gov.uk/media/6411a602e90e0776996a4ade/national_quantum_strategy.pdf

DSIT (Department for Science, Innovation and Technology). (2023b). *National Quantum Strategy Missions*. https://www.gov.uk/government/publications/national-quantum-strategy/national-quantum-strategy-missions

Ehrenfest, P. (1911). Welche Züge der Lichtquantenhypothese spielen in der Theorie der Wärmestrahlung eine wesentliche Rolle? *Annalen der Physik, 36*, 91–118.

Einstein, A. (1905). Über einen die Erzeugung und Verwandlung des Lichtes betreffenden heuristischen Gesichtspunkt" *Annalen der Physik, 17*, 132–148.

Fuenfschilling, L., & Binz, C. (2018). Global socio-technical regimes. *Research Policy, 47*(4), 735–749.

Geels, F. W. (2002). Technological transitions as evolutionary reconfiguration processes: A multi-level perspective and a case-study. *Research Policy, 31*(8–9), 1257–1274.

Geels, F. W. (2012). A socio-technical analysis of low-carbon transitions: Introducing the multi-level perspective into transport studies. *Journal of Transport Geography, 24*, 471–482.

Geels, F. W. (2014). Regime resistance against low-carbon transitions: Introducing politics and power into the multi-level perspective. *Theory, Culture & Society, 31*(5), 21–40.

Geels, F. W. (2019). Socio-technical transitions to sustainability: A review of criticisms and elaborations of the multi-level perspective. *Current Opinion in Environmental Sustainability, 39*, 187–201.

Geels, F. W., & Schot, J. (2007). Typology of sociotechnical transition pathways. *Research Policy, 36*(3), 399–417.

GOS (Government Office for Science). (2016). *The quantum age: Technological opportunities.* https://assets.publishing.service.gov.uk/media/5a81828c40f0b62302697b29/gs-16-18-quantum-technologies-report.pdf

Heisenberg, W. (1925). Über quantentheoretische Umdeutung kinematischer und mechanischer Beziehungen". *Zeitschrift Für Physik, 33*, 879–893.

Hess, D. J. (2023). Conflict and uneven development in the multidecade distributed solar energy transition in the United States. *Proceedings of the National Academy of Sciences, 120*(47), Article e2206200119.

Knight, P. (2019, May). *Interview in Engineering & Technology, 14*(4), 30–33.

Levin, F. S. (2002). *An introduction to quantum theory.* Cambridge University Press.

MacDougall, R. (2006). Long lines: AT&T's long-distance network as an organisational and political strategy. *The Business History Review, 80*(2), 297–327.

McKinsey. (2024). *Quantum technology monitor April 2024.* https://www.mckinsey.com/capabilities/mckinsey-digital/our-insights/steady-progress-in-approaching-the-quantum-advantage

OECD. (2015). *Digital economy outlook 2015.* OECD Publishing.

Planck, M. (1901). Ueber die Elementarquanta der Materie und der Elektricität. *Annalen der Physik, 309*, 553–566.

QED-C. (2023). *4th Annual QC global market forecast.* https://quantumconsortium.org/4th-annual-qc-global-market-forecast/

Qureca. (2023). *Overview of quantum initiatives worldwide 2023.* https://qureca.com/overview-of-quantum-initiatives-worldwide-2023/

RAE. (2024). *Royal academy of engineering quantum infrastructure review.* https://raeng.org.uk/media/rrqjm2v3/quantum-infrastructure-review.pdf

Rip, A., & Kemp, R. (1998). Technological change. In *Human choice and climate change: Vol. II, Resources and Technology* (pp. 327–300). Battelle Press.

Ryghaug, M., & Skjølsvold, T. M. (2023). How policies and actor strategies affect electric vehicle diffusion and wider sustainability transitions. *Proceedings of the National Academy of Sciences, 120*(47), Article e2207888119.

Schrödinger, E. (1926). An undulatory theory of the mechanics of atoms and molecules. *Physical Review, 28*(6), 1049–1070.

Schrödinger, E. (1935). Discussion of probability Relations between separated systems. *Mathematical Proceedings of the Cambridge Philosophical Society, 31*(4), 555–563.

Sodhi, M. S., & Tayur, S. R. (2022). Make your business quantum-ready today. *Management and Business Review, 2*(2), 78–84.

Ten Holter, C., Jirotka, M., & Inglesant, P. (2021). *Creating a responsible quantum future: the case for a dedicated national resource for responsible quantum computing*. University of Oxford.

Tushman, M. L., & Anderson, P. (1986). Technological discontinuities and organizational environment. *Administrative Science Quarterly*, 439–465.

Utterback, J. M. (1996). *Mastering the dynamics of innovation*. Harvard Business School Press.

Utterback, J. M., & Abernathy, W. J. (1975). A dynamic model of process and product innovation. *Omega, 3*(6), 639–656.

Utterback, J. M., & Suárez, F. F. (1993). Innovation, competition, and industry structure. *Research Policy, 22*(1), 1–21.

Velu, C. (2016). Evolutionary or revolutionary business model innovation through coopetition? The role of dominance in network markets. *Industrial Marketing Management, 53*, 124–135.

Velu, C. (2017). A systems perspective on business model evolution: The case of an agricultural information service provider in India. *Long Range Planning, 50*(5), 603–620.

Velu, C. (2018). Coopetition and business models. In *Routledge companion to coopetition strategies* (pp. 336–346). Routledge.

Velu, C. (2024). *Business model innovation: A blueprint for strategic change*. Cambridge University Press.

Velu, C., & Jacob, A. (2016). Business model innovation and owner–managers: The moderating role of competition. *R&D Management, 46*(3), 451–463.

Velu, C., & Putra, F. H. (2023). How to introduce quantum computers without slowing economic growth. *Nature, 619*(7970), 461–464.

Zott, C., & Amit, R. (2010). Business model design: An activity system perspective. *Long Range Planning, 43*(2–3), 216–226.

Zott, C., Amit, R., & Massa, L. (2011). The business model: Recent developments and future research. *Journal of Management, 37*(4), 1019–1042.

CHAPTER 2

Quantum Computers and Computing a Better World

This chapter covers:

- *An overview of the concepts of quantum computers and their potential breakthroughs for society and industry;*
- *How do quantum computers work? Some intuitive explanations;*
- *An outline of experiments that firms are already doing using prototype quantum computers to explore business problems;*
- *The UK National Quantum Technologies Programme, other national programmes, and funding;*
- *Some basic principles of quantum mechanics and why they provide economic and societal benefits;*
- *A discussion of the possible business and economic implications using the frameworks outlined in Chapter 1;*
- *An outline of research questions to be explored further.*

Introduction

Quantum computing is an emerging technology. At the time of writing, no quantum computer in the world can outperform a classical computer in a business setting. No quantum computer can yet perform a business calculation faster than a standard laptop. No quantum computer can optimise an industrial process more efficiently than a moderately powered smartphone. So why is there so much interest in quantum

C. Velu et al., *The Business of Quantum Technologies*,
https://doi.org/10.1007/978-3-031-99808-9_2

computing? Why are so many governments investing in developing national quantum computing initiatives? And why should industry be thinking about implementing quantum machines in the coming years?

First, as Feynman identified in the 1980s, there is a class of simulation problems that can never, in principle, be carried out accurately on a classical computer. Quoting Feynman, "...how we can simulate with a computer [...] quantum–mechanical effects. If you have a single particle...this could be simulated... But the full description of quantum mechanics for a large system has too many variables, [and] it cannot be simulated with a normal computer" (Feynman, 1982).

Second, over the last two decades, the world has become increasingly digital, with a growing prevalence of data (e.g., through sensors and other behavioural data sources from digital interactions), and more reliant on precisely these technologies, which have a natural limit at atomic scales. The boundaries of these technologies are already being pushed, and for many applications, these technologies are at a natural limit.

Third, there is a natural limit to how much the current "classical" microprocessors can be miniaturised. "Moore's law" expresses the growth of the possible number of components that can be fitted onto a silicon chip as a function of time, which has been observed to roughly double every 2 years (Fig. 2.1). Moore's law is not expected to continue indefinitely, as the components of current chip designs are approaching atomic sizes, beyond which there is no practical way to produce an electronic component on a two-dimensional chip (Courtland, 2015). That said, there may be other innovations in classical computing, but there will still be a class of problems that can never be solved classically, even if solutions are found for further miniaturisation of the chips.

It is likely that quantum computing will be complementary to digital computers and used to perform complex calculations. For example, quantum computers are likely to be used to enable some optimisation problems and possibly enhance machine learning and artificial intelligence.

What Is a Computer? Bits and Logic Gates

In the context of this book, a computer is simply a device for processing data. Data come in many forms—the words in this book, numbers, pictures, sound, movies—and a computer is essentially a machine that stores data, retrieves that data, processes it, and outputs it. These tasks

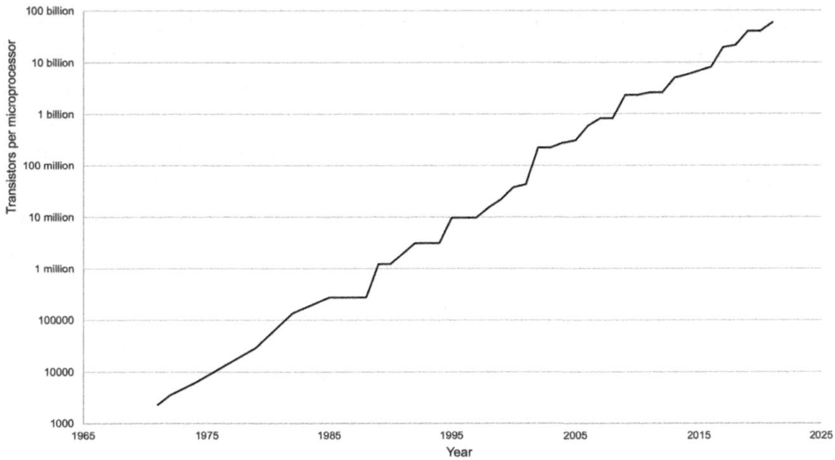

Fig. 2.1 Moore's law: Number of transistors per microprocessor by year (*Source* Karl Rupp, Microprocessor Trend Data (2022). Adapted from OurWorldIn-Data.org/technological-change (2022) CC-BY

can be implemented in many ways. An ancient abacus can be thought of as a computer—the beads on the wires can be set in a way that represents numbers that are stored and retrieved by noting their positions on the wires, processed by sliding the beads along the wires to represent a mathematical operation (say, addition), and then read out.

Most modern computers, of course, have electronic circuits implemented on silicon chips rather than beads on wires. Data storage on a modern computer is accomplished with dedicated memory, which can be written to and read from, and data is processed by implementing software algorithms on that data. Output might be to a screen, a sound card, or another software algorithm. But the principle of a computer as a data-processing machine is common, whether that computer is a laptop, a tablet, or an abacus.

Modern computers represent all data as a series of 1s and 0s, represented in digital circuits as "on" (1) and "off" (0). There are no halfway values; the 1s and 0s are referred to as "binary digits" or, more typically, "bits". By building sequences of bits, essentially any form of data can be represented. For example, the sequence 01000111 might represent the character "G" in a text document, and the sequence

000000001111111100000000 might represent the colour green in an image file—both of these examples are used widely in computing.

Software processes the sequences of bits appropriately for whatever data they represent and outputs the results of that processing, either to the user or potentially back into storage. This processing is carried out by very simple circuits called *logic gates*, which operate on one or two bits at the same time. Examples of logic gates include the NOT gate (which changes an input of 0 to an output of 1, and an input of 1 to an output of 0), the AND gate (which compares two inputs, and outputs 0 if the inputs are 00, 01, or 10, and 1 if the inputs are 11), and the OR gate (which outputs 0 if the inputs are 00, and 1 if the inputs are 01, 10, or 11). By combining logic gates, classical computers can perform simple arithmetic operations, from which more complex operations can be built up.

The Historical Perspective

The advancement of digital computing has a long history, often traced back to the early 1820s when Charles Babbage, the "Father of Computing", developed a design for an early mechanical calculator, the Difference Engine. Subsequently, in 1837, Babbage designed the Analytical Engine, which laid many of the conceptual foundations of the modern digital computer. Alan Turing later made seminal contributions, including his conceptual Turing Machine in the 1930s (Bromley, 1982). His ideas led to the breaking of encrypted codes during World War II, demonstrating the application of digital computing in the cryptography domain. In the USA, Claude Shannon was also working on cryptanalysis, and shortly after the war he published his mathematical theory of communications (Shannon, 1948), laying the foundations for information theory. Digital computers were further advanced by IT firms such as IBM and then commercialised into business applications. For instance, LEO (Lyons Electronic Office), originally implemented in the UK by J. Lyons and Co. in the early 1950s, was one of the first commercially successful computers, the world's first integrated information-management system used to calculate daily production requirements and document management (Frank, 2022). LEO was initially used to improve the production and management of bakery items at the Lyons Tea shops across the UK.

From these beginnings, digital computers contributed to changing processes and workflows in the manufacturing industry, and they increased the productivity of production systems (Cortada, 2004). In the early stage of adoption (the 1960s–70s), digital computers enabled firms to digitise data collection on shop-floor activities and to share coordinated information about those activities with other departments. Following this digitisation, computer-integrated manufacturing (CIM) systems improved the coordination of activities across the enterprise, including procurement, production, and distribution. In addition, computer-aided design (CAD) improved product design and simulation of materials, which facilitated better product customisation. By the 1990s, the internet was beginning to globally connect digital computers, which led to new business models such as just-in-time production and mass customisation through flexible manufacturing systems (Cortada, 2004).

However, when digital computers gained popularity in the 1970s and 1980s, rather than delivering efficiencies for 15 years they slowed growth in productivity (the value-added relative to inputs such as labour) by 0.76% per annum (Velu & Putra, 2023). Such a dip is known as the productivity paradox, which arose because businesses had to invest in new equipment and learn how to program the devices, as well as working out what to use them for. At first, firms did not invest enough in the other innovations needed to change core processes and business models (Brynjolfsson & Hitt, 2003; Wannakrairoj & Velu, 2021). Only after several sectors had adjusted in the 1990s did productivity growth rise again.

Moreover, in the retail sector, it took Walmart a decade of investment in digital computing to be able to share data with its supply chain and hence optimise production and distribution. These changes required new business models, which contributed to productivity growth after a period of slowdown. Hence, a recent study argued that the adoption of quantum computing could result in a slowdown of productivity growth because of the "steep learning curve" that industries might face adapting to the technology and developing new business models (Velu & Putra, 2023).

There are three reasons for this steep learning curve. First, there is the incremental benefit relative to costs for most firms, as they tend to think about using quantum computers for marginal applications, based on existing business problems. Digital computers replaced electromechanical machines, which meant there were very few integration costs. However, quantum computers will work in conjunction with, and complementary to, digital computers. So, there will be a larger integration cost than when digital computers materialised. As a result, it is likely that productivity will slow down for some time before more radical applications are identified that add significant value. To address this, mission-driven or society-level challenges need to be defined for quantum computers with the aid of government funding in order to attract private investment. For example, such mission-driven propositions could include weather forecasting, resilient financial systems, or developing low-carbon technologies to address climate change, where the problem is industry-wide or societal. A proof of concept could then be shown, and private-sector firms could scale it up.

The second reason for the steep learning curve is cognitive drag. Digital computers are relatively easy to understand. However, quantum computers based on the principles of quantum mechanics are not that intuitive. So, the translation cost between scientists, engineers, and business managers will be much higher than for digital computers. We need to address this by providing translation aids such as shared language and artefacts that enable knowledge sharing, so that scientists, engineers, and business managers can use a common language and translate digital to quantum—and back again—seamlessly.

The third reason is that most firms will look at the chance of a cryptographic break, whereby quantum computers are likely to be able to decode many of the cryptographic systems in place. Firms will initially tend to be defensive to protect themselves against these cryptographic costs. Building a quantum-enabled network structure—or the quantum internet—could overcome this security threat and spur growth across many industries, as the creation of the original internet did.

Although the digital computer has undoubtedly improved productivity and enabled new business models, there are certain classes of problem for which digital computation is limited, preventing the emergence of new value propositions (Paudel et al., 2022).

What Is a Quantum Computer? Qubits and Quantum Logic

Let us recall our discussion in Chapter 1, where we described the quantum properties of superposition and entanglement. There, we discussed an analogy of typical quantum states as being like a spinning coin—quantum states are generally a mixture of "heads" and "tails", until we measure that state. At the point that we do that, we always find either heads *or* tails, never both, just as grabbing a spinning coin out of the air forces it into one state. We now begin to see how a quantum state might help us to build a computational device: given the preceding discussion on digital computers, we see that a quantum state also has an analogue with classical bits. However, we should be aware of a clear difference between quantum states and classical bits—classical bits are only ever 0 or 1, while quantum systems are generally a superposition of multiple possible states, until they are measured.

If we take the simplest quantum system, we will generally find it in a mixture of states. We previously referred to heads and tails, but we could also have described it as a mixture of 0 and 1. We thus see how a two-state quantum system could, in principle, be used as a computational bit, but the superposition principle means *a single quantum bit can represent more information than a single classical bit*. Bear in mind that when we measure it, we will only ever observe 0 or 1 from a quantum bit, but its general state is a superposition of both 0 and 1.

In Chapter 1, we also introduced the idea of entanglement, where multiple quantum objects can only be fully described by a single, shared state. Given an array of multiple qubits, we can engineer an entangled state where all the qubits share a single quantum state. By manipulating this state in a single operation, we manipulate every entangled qubit simultaneously. Importantly, adding just *one* more qubit *doubles* the processing power of the array. It is this principle that gives quantum computers their huge advantage over classical machines. A few hundred perfectly reliable entangled qubits could represent more numbers than there are atoms in the entire universe. Manipulating an array of such entangled qubits with a quantum equivalent of logic gates would enable us to process vast amounts of data in a single operation.

But we should be wary. Remember that when we measure the state of a quantum object, we never see a superposition of states—like grabbing a spinning coin from the air, we only ever observe heads or tails, never both. When we come to read out the state of an entangled array of qubits, we never find the array in an entangled superposition—instead we find each qubit in a well-defined state. So how has this helped? This is where the art of developing quantum algorithms comes in. It turns out that it is possible to develop quantum algorithms that can preferentially move an entangled array of quantum objects into a desired end state, without knowing a priori the details of that end state. If the desired end state is the solution to some problem, the final (measured) entangled array of quantum objects will have "solved" that problem. Not every problem is amenable to such quantum algorithms, but over the last three decades several algorithms have been developed with the potential to solve real-world problems, which we will examine later in this chapter. A simplified introduction to a prototype quantum algorithm is provided in Box 1.

Box 1: An Introductory Quantum Algorithm What follows is a variant of Economou et al.' (2020) "Tiger and Money" story, which demonstrated the technical computing process, with a simplified explanation, and loosely based on Deutsch and Josza (1992).

The set-up of the game is shown in Fig. 2.2. There are two sealed boxes, and a button opens both boxes simultaneously. It is not possible to open only one box, but we know there is money in at least one box. We also know there may or may not be a tiger in one of the boxes. If you push the button and open the boxes and find there is no tiger, you keep the money. However, if you push the button and there is a tiger in either box, it eats you before you can get the money, so it is important to determine whether or not there is a tiger in either of the boxes. Fortunately, there is a classical computer next to the boxes that is programmed to answer truthfully to simple yes/no questions about the presence of a tiger.

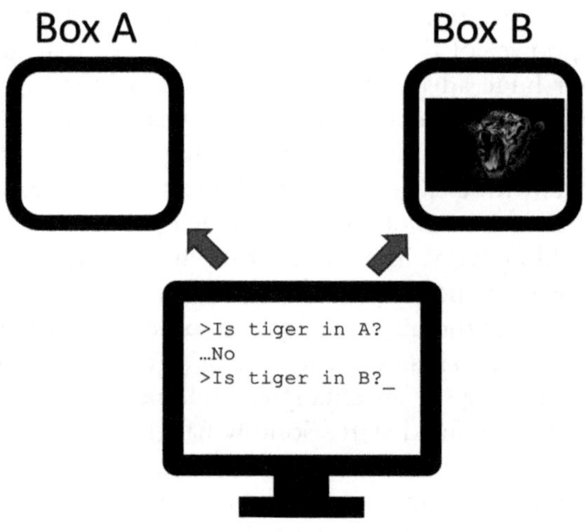

Fig. 2.2 Tiger and money game

How many questions do we need to ask the computer to ensure there is no tiger? We might get lucky, but we will generally need to ask *two* questions for *two* boxes. If there were 1000 boxes, we would need to ask 1,000 questions to ensure there were no tiger. We could programme the computer to do this, and we might get "lucky" early on, but the number of yes/no questions generally scales with the number of boxes. In this example more boxes mean more time spent on the computation.

What happens if we replace our simple digital computer with a quantum computer running a quantum algorithm? We can represent the boxes using two qubits. Using quantum superposition, we can arrange our qubits to simultaneously represent the state of "There is no tiger" (0) and "There is a tiger" (1). The quantum algorithm for two boxes is:

(1) Prepare two qubits, each representing a box, and put them in superposition.
(2) Entangle these qubits.
(3) Reapply superposition to the entangled qubits and query the final state.

From the results of the measurement, we can infer whether or not there is a tiger. Our quantum computer can make just one query of our two-qubit system and return *with certainty* whether there is a tiger (depending on the details, the quantum mechanical result may be 100% certain, or very close to 100% certain). The combination of the superposition and entanglement operations encodes additional information about the presence of the tiger; specifically, entanglement allows us to infer the state of one qubit by reading the state of the other. If we had 1000 boxes, we could effectively use our quantum algorithm to tell us whether there were a tiger in any of those 1,000 boxes in a single query. This reduction in the number of queries increases the speed of the quantum computation over the classical computation.

While this problem is pedagogical, it highlights the advantage of quantum algorithms over classical algorithms in some cases. Each quantum query might be slower than a classical one, and, in the case of two boxes, a classical algorithm may well outperform a quantum one. However, as the size of the problem increases (in our analogy, as we add more boxes), for problems of this nature there is a "tipping point" where quantum algorithms, in principle, become much more efficient than classical ones, leading to significant speed-ups in computing time.

An Alternative Quantum Computer—Quantum Simulation

In addition to the quantum logic algorithms and hardware introduced above, there is another way of thinking about quantum computing that is closer to Feynman's original conception. The quantum computers described can be said to be general-purpose machines, in the sense that they can perform any computation that a classical computer can perform; and, as we have seen in some cases, they may be able to perform these calculations more efficiently than a classical computer. Feynman's original idea was to use quantum mechanics to simulate nature, using simple quantum mechanical systems to simulate more complex quantum mechanical systems.

We can use another classical analogy to explain how this might work. Consider blowing soap bubbles—the shape of the bubble is determined by the interaction of the surface tension of the soap, and the pressure of the air inside and outside the bubble. This is generally a well-understood physical model, which is described mathematically in terms of the energy stored in the soap film. However, this can be a tedious calculation, depending on the circumstances. The simple case is to blow a spherical bubble from a point source. This is potentially easy to model in terms of air pressure and energy stored in the surface tension of the soap. But what about more complicated cases where three-dimensional shapes are dipped in a soap bath? What shape will the soap film take? Rather than performing potentially complicated mathematical calculations, a simple solution is to try it out with a real 3D wire frame in a bath of soap and observe what shape the soap film adopts. In a sense, the soap film performs the energy calculations for us. Similarly, to model complex quantum mechanical systems, we can build simpler quantum analogues and let them evolve over time to see what energy configurations they adopt. Instead of building a direct mathematical model of the system, we have modelled the complex system directly into a similar physical system, and then observed how it behaves over time, to infer how the more complex system might behave over time. This exploration of an "energy landscape" (i.e. letting a system evolve over time is the equivalent of a soap-film 3D wire frame) is known as *quantum annealing*.

The challenge in this context is to find a mapping between the system of interest and a quantum mechanical version of the 3D wire frame in a soap bath. Technically, this corresponds to identifying an appropriate energy landscape that we wish to explore with our quantum system. This is not always possible for general systems—this form of quantum computing cannot be applied to every system that we might wish to model. However, for several problems, such as cargo-packing optimisation, or certain problems in drug discovery, quantum annealing approaches have been applied with some success.

Building a Quantum Computer

There has been huge progress over the course of the last decade or so in terms of engineering reliable qubits. At the start of the 2010s, university researchers could generate one or two qubits and maintain them for a short period. Over the next 10 years, research moved out of the lab and into industry, and by early 2024 at least two 1,000-qubit machines had been announced, with some companies publicly laying out timelines for further developments in the coming years.

Unlike classical hardware, which is essentially based on our ability to engineer silicon chips, there are several competing approaches to quantum computing hardware. The most widely adopted approach in industry—used by IBM and Google—relies on the properties of so-called "superconducting" materials when they are cooled down to very low temperatures, typically of the order of 1,000 times lower than the temperature of deep space. Other approaches involve trapping charged particles using lasers, or engineering the crystal structures of lab-grown diamonds to have appropriate quantum mechanical properties. Some researchers and industrial organisations are actively pursuing the use of silicon engineered in the same way as in chip production. See Table 2.1 for a summary of different hardware modalities for quantum computers.

Meanwhile, work has progressed on the hardware to control these qubits. It is interesting to note that while quantum thermodynamic considerations suggest that quantum computers may have lower power resource requirements than classical machines (particularly for calculations that use fewer steps than classical calculations), the classical control hardware around the quantum processor may have significant power resource requirements (Auffèves, 2022). Tools have also been developed to entangle qubits and then manipulate them with the quantum equivalents of classical logic gates. These quantum gates typically do not have exact analogues in the classical computing world, but they generally

Table 2.1 Hardware modalities of quantum computers

Modality	*Qubit Representation*	*Advantages*	*Disadvantages*
Superconducting	Electrical current in superconducting loops	Mature technology, good scalability, relatively high speed	Requires extremely low temperatures, and decoherence is an issue
Trapped ion	Individual ions held by electric fields	Mature technology, long coherence times, high-fidelity operations	Harder to scale
Neutral atoms	Neutral atoms trapped by lasers and magnetic fields	Long coherence times, potentially scalable	Less mature technology (but developing rapidly)
Photonic	Light pulses in optical fibres	Can transmit information over long distances, potentially scalable	Short coherence times
Quantum dots	Electrons confined in semiconductors	Potentially compatible with existing silicon technology and manufacturing	Short coherence times
Nitrogen-vacancy centres	Defects in diamond crystals	Long coherence times at room temperature	Less mature technology
Topological qubits	Exotic materials	Potentially inherently fault-tolerant, long coherence times	Very early stage of development, less research activity in this area

Source Authors

modify the quantum-state parameters of the qubits according to a defined quantum algorithm. A second class of tools is used in quantum simulators to set up qubits in a lattice and then effectively let them evolve to their lowest energy.

Nonetheless, we are still some years away from a quantum computer that would challenge a classical computer, even for problems that are particularly suited to quantum processing. Despite the advances of the last decade, we have yet to generate enough high-quality qubits to overcome the challenge of them interacting with their environment. This environmental interaction is termed "noise", and the current best-in-class quantum machines are often referred to as "noisy intermediate-scale quantum" (NISQ) computers (Preskill, 2018). How will this noise be overcome?

Remarkably, scientists have developed a process of quantum error correction. The fact that this is even possible is striking: the act of checking whether a qubit has changed its state as a result of noise typically involves reading out the state of that qubit. As noted above, this would destroy any superposition of states that qubit might be in, leaving it in a single state dependent on the laws of probability (remember we only ever observe heads or tails, each with a probability of 50%, rather than a superposition of both heads and tails). However, scientists have proposed a quantum method of correcting qubit errors. Instead of coding information into a single physical qubit, quantum error correction invokes a larger group of qubits, together acting as a "logical qubit". Logical qubits provide redundancy in case a single qubit gets corrupted, and logical qubits can be monitored for errors and corrected if a corruption occurs.

This redundancy in logical qubits comes at a cost—building error-correcting logical qubits requires many physical qubits. Estimates suggest that at least the order of tens of thousands of physical qubits will be required before fully fault-tolerant quantum computers are realised; and, realistically, for many quantum applications, we will need hundreds of thousands—to millions—of physical qubits before reaching an advantage over classical machines.

Is this scale achievable? Doubts have been raised over the last two decades about whether this scale of machine is realisable (e.g., Kalai, 2016). Lab-based machines typically have tens of physical qubits rather than tens of thousands. However, the pace of change has been rapid. In the early 2020s, several companies have released quantum machines with hundreds of qubits, and some organisations are publishing timelines for when they expect to reach a realistic number of physical qubits required for fault tolerance. Although there are no guarantees, achieving fault tolerance by the end of the 2020s may be possible.

Quantum Algorithms

Hardware aside, another element of quantum computation is often overlooked in elementary discussions. The link between quantum hardware and applications is the development over the last 30 years of quantum algorithms. An algorithm is a mathematical procedure for transforming data, which takes some input, applies a procedure, and generates some output. Quantum algorithms use the properties of superposition and entanglement to transform the state of qubits, and they generally provide a method for finding the right solution to a problem from the very large number of states represented by an array of qubits. This is a key difference from classical algorithms, which generally map one set of inputs to a unique set of outputs. Quantum algorithms map one set of inputs to a set of entangled quantum states in superposition (representing, in principle, a very large set of possible outputs), and then evolve these quantum states so that the desired outputs are amplified and "wrong answers" suppressed.

The fact this is even possible is surprising—and that several algorithms have been discovered that can employ this technique is remarkable. The interested reader should consult the Quantum Algorithm Zoo (2024) for a well-maintained list of such methods. There are many dozens of such algorithms, although not all of them appear to have practical applications. However, several algorithms are expected to be useful for real-world needs. Of these, two are particularly noteworthy. First, Shor's algorithm has become something of a poster child for quantum computing. It can find the factors of large integers much faster than the best classical algorithms. In principle, this poses a significant threat to current internet security, which depends on the difficulty of finding the factors of large numbers, although in practice, new classical methods have been discovered that are resistant to Shor's algorithm. Second, Grover's algorithm is a quantum technique used to find specific data in very large, unsorted lists, and it has potential applications in pattern matching and general optimisation. Algorithms like Shor's algorithm scale very rapidly with problem size and become much more efficient than classical algorithms, even for moderately sized problems (in the case of Shor's algorithm, for moderately large numbers). Other quantum algorithms, such as Grover's algorithm, do not scale as quickly with problem size—they are only likely to provide advantage for very large problems (in the case of Grover's algorithm, for very large data sets). Nevertheless, even methods like Grover's algorithm are expected to solve problems that the fastest conceivable classical computers are unlikely ever to solve in areas such as security, materials science, chemistry, pharmaceuticals, finance, and defence. The fact that quantum computers will be able to do things that classical computers are unlikely to be able to do raises interesting questions about benchmarking these new technologies. Beyond the technical characterisation of the performance of a quantum computer (e.g., the fidelity of its gate operations), how does one benchmark the performance of an algorithm implemented on a particular piece of hardware when there is no clear baseline to benchmark against? How does one know that the algorithm has given the correct answer to a problem when there is no classical calculation to compare it with? What metrics need to be developed? These questions are the subject of active research programmes (e.g., Proctor et al., 2024).

Box 2: A Primer for Shor's Algorithm Shor's algorithm, developed by Peter Shor in 1994, is a quantum algorithm used to efficiently factor large integers. This is important in cryptography, where security is based on the difficulty finding the factors of large numbers. Recall that, in general, a number is factorised by the integer numbers that must be multiplied together to generate the original number. For example, factors of 15 are 5 and 3. Recall also that prime numbers are those with no factors other than themselves and 1, such as 17 (no two integers can be multiplied together to make 17, other than 1 and 17, so 17 is a prime number). The prime factors of an integer are thus prime numbers that are factors of that integer. In the example of the number 15, $5 \times 3 = 15$, and 5 and 3 are both prime numbers; hence, they are the prime factors of 15.

There is an interesting fact about multiplying two prime numbers together, which is useful in this context. Using 15 as our example, let us consider the remainder when we divide 2 by 15: $2/15 = 0$ remainder 2. Now divide 2^2 by 15, so $4/15 = 0$ remainder 4. Now try 2^3 by 15, so $8/15 = 0$ remainder 8. Continue this sequence, finding $16/15 = 1$ remainder 1, $32/15 = 2$ remainder 2, $64/15 = 4$ remainder 4, $128/15 = 8$ remainder 8, $256/15 = 17$ remainder 1, and so on. We are only interested in the remainders, so in the above calculations we see a series of remainders emerging: 2, 4, 8, 1, 2, 4, 8, ... In fact, if we had begun our calculations with 2^0 (= 1) instead of 2^1 (= 2), our sequence of remainders would run 1, 2, 4, 8, 1, 2, 4, 8, 1, 2, 4, 8, ... We see a repeating pattern of 1, 2, 4, 8. We say that the *period* of this sequence is 4—there are four numbers before the sequence starts repeating in this example. It turns out that for any integer, N, which is the product of two prime numbers, p and q, the sequence

$$x \bmod N,\ x^2 \bmod N,\ x^3 \bmod N,\ x^4 \bmod N,\ \ldots$$

will repeat with some period that evenly divides $(p-1).(q-1)$ for any integer x that is not divisible by p or q. The upshot of this is that *learning the period of the repeating sequence gives some information about* $(p-1).(q-1)$. If we tried different values of x, we would learn even more about $(p-1).(q-1)$, and for enough trials of different x we might be able to calculate the actual value of $(p-1).(q-1)$. Given that, we might be able to find p and q, the prime numbers we are interested in. Now, for a classical computer, finding the period is still a difficult calculation, so this method cannot help us to find prime factors using classical computation. However, note that the period is now a property, not of each element in the sequence but of the sequence taken as a whole. A quantum computer could represent this idea by creating a superposition of all the elements of x mod N, x^2 mod N, x^3 mod N, … and then performing some algorithm on that whole superposition. What form would this algorithm take? If you have studied some mathematics or data science, the idea of extracting a period, or equivalently a frequency of some sort from a set of data, is reminiscent of Fourier transforms (FTs). FTs turn input data, in terms of a signal that varies with time, into output data composed of frequencies. Just as a prism splits white light into its constituent colours, an FT splits an input signal into its constituent frequencies. To find the period of our quantum superposition, we need a quantum Fourier transform (QFT), which will take our input periodic quantum state and transform it into a new quantum state that represents the frequencies (and hence periods) in the original state. QFTs have been widely studied and can be implemented on existing quantum computers. Once the QFT has been carried out, the computation can be re-run using different values of x, which can be used in classical computations to generate possible values for $(p-1)$ x $(q-1)$, and thus p and q. The power of Shor's algorithm lies in its ability to exploit quantum mechanics to solve the period-finding problem efficiently. The time that Shor's algorithm takes to factor a large integer N scales favourably with the size of N, which is generally a significant speed-up compared to classical factoring algorithms.

Beyond Shor's and Grover's quantum algorithms, a range of hybrid classical–quantum algorithms are likely to benefit some problems, possibly in the medium term. For example, the variational quantum eigensolver has been used to calculate the ground states of molecules, relying on combining quantum algorithms with classical methods (Peruzzo et al. 2014).

In Box 2, we provide a simplified primer for Shor's algorithm.

Business Case Studies

We now move from a description of the technology to look at some of the business issues surrounding quantum computing. The naïve expectation might be that only established IT vendors would be able to capitalise on these nascent hardware and algorithm technologies as they emerge from academic research. It is true that IBM, Google, Microsoft, Amazon, and other established international players have dedicated quantum programmes, and they are making significant technical developments. However, in the last 10 years, there has been a surge in new quantum computing businesses, both in the hardware and algorithm spaces, and a few of these new companies have already been purchased by more established organisations.

Despite the lack of advantage that current quantum hardware provides over classical computers, many companies are already experimenting with the available technology. With the possible exception of quantum random number generation (which is well established as a principle and now has vendors offering true random number generation as a service), one should view all these experiments as early-stage testing of ideas about how quantum computing might be beneficial in the future. We emphasise that no quantum computer can currently outperform a classical machine in these types of task, and none of these case studies has led to a substantial advantage over classical computing—they are exploring what might be possible in the coming years. Moreover, there is some ongoing research on the energy efficiency of quantum computing, which might incentivise firms to explore the technology for computation for sustainability considerations (Auffèves, 2022). However, even in the short term, they indicate where industry might be looking to use quantum computation in the future. We next provide an overview of some of the use cases in quantum computing for simulation, optimisation, and quantum machine-learning applications.

Simulation Case Studies

BMW and Airbus

One of the major challenges facing the aerospace sector is the need to decarbonise the fleet (Cazzola & Lassman, 2021). The existing aircraft fleet in the aerospace sector has a significant carbon footprint from using carbon-based fuel such as kerosene. There will be a large increase in demand for narrow-bodied aircraft from international passenger travel over the next decade. Hence, Airbus is working on the next-generation fuel-cell-based aircraft. These next-generation aircraft will be based on hydrogen fuel cells and will have no carbon or nitrogen dioxide emissions. In order to achieve the tight timeline for delivering the first prototype of these aircraft by 2026, Airbus is working closely with BMW to simulate the fuel cell development using quantum computers (Airbus, 2024). The simulations require complex modelling of the efficiency of fuel cells using hydrogen as a source of energy. The simulation uses advanced quantum chemistry to capture the correlations of the molecules and their combinations using the processing power of early-prototype quantum computers.

Bosch

Bosch is a German multinational engineering and technology company that works on the global supply of high technology and services across many automotive industries. One significant issue encountered by Bosch is simulating functional materials relevant to fuel cells, batteries, or electric engines that contain strongly correlated electrons. The conventional classical techniques have limited accuracy in simulating the properties of these materials. Therefore, in 2022, Bosch started working closely with IBM and partnering on a strategic quantum computing engagement to jointly develop quantum computing applications in the material science domain in the context of electromobility, renewable energy, and sensor technology (Bosch, 2022; IBM, 2022).

Experts from both companies are sharing expertise and resources and co-investigating quantum computing applications. Bosch provides industrial experience in simulating materials with classical computers, as well as expertise and capabilities on mass technology production. IBM provides quantum computing technologies, including its Qiskit Runtime, and expertise in developing and implementing quantum algorithms in industry. The joint work has encompassed many areas of activity, including hardware, software, and ecosystem development, and workflows ranging from realistic modelling of materials to scaling up commercial interest. Bosch is also actively engaging with the European Quantum Industry Consortium (QuIC) and the German Quantum Technology and Application Consortium (QUTAC) and participating in many national and international quantum projects and committees.

Volkswagen Group

The Volkswagen Group is a German multinational manufacturing company delivering passenger and commercial vehicles, motorcycles, engines, and turbomachinery. One important issue facing Volkswagen is developing cost-effective and sustainable batteries, which requires accurate and reliable simulations of battery materials, beyond the abilities of current classical techniques. Volkswagen has engaged with quantum computing providers such as Xanadu, a Canadian provider, and they are co-exploring the industrial potential of quantum computing using Xanadu's next-generation quantum computer (Volkswagen, 2022), with which they have simulated the key properties of lithium-ion batteries (Delgado et al., 2022). Volkswagen has also signed a memorandum of understanding with the Canadian government to advance e-mobility in Canada. The Canadian government has invested heavily in quantum technologies, with the aim of involving global talent to build up a quantum ecosystem to develop and advance Canada's battery supply chain.

Rolls-Royce

Rolls-Royce is investigating materials development using quantum computing techniques. The firm has partnered with Riverlane and the National Quantum Computing Centre on work to reduce the number of qubits that might be needed to simulate materials on a quantum computer, potentially leading to lighter, stronger materials for jet engines (NQCC, 2023). Rolls-Royce is also investigating the use of quantum computers for computational fluid dynamics (CFD) applications—and the company has worked with NVIDIA and Classiq to simulate quantum computing circuits for use in CFD (IoTWorldToday, 2023).

Biogen

Biogen is an American multinational biotechnology company. The discovery of a new drug therapy generally takes more than 10 years, at significant cost, as multiple molecules need to be tested. Current digital computers can simulate some small molecules but are not suited to simulating larger numbers of atoms. Quantum computers are expected to be able to model much larger molecules using the principles of quantum mechanics. Biogen has collaborated with Accenture Labs and 1QBit (a Canadian quantum software firm) to co-develop quantum-enabled structural molecular comparison, helping with drug discovery for complex conditions like multiple sclerosis, Alzheimer's, Parkinson's, and Lou Gehrig's disease (Pharmaphorum, 2017).

Optimisation Case Studies

Airbus

Airbus is working to reduce the time it takes to load aircraft with cargo, while improving packing efficiency (Airbus, 2024). There are different combinations of package size, and the availability of containers in which to load them is constantly changing. This is the so-called "knapsack problem"—how to identify the best combination of parcels to load in each container as quickly as possible—and it is typically difficult for digital computers to find an optimal solution. Small improvements in efficiency could save airports and logistics firms a significant amount of money and contribute to fuel efficiency, thus reducing the environmental impact. Airbus has been working with IonQ, a US quantum computer firm, on "toy" versions of this problem, demonstrating the potential to decrease the computation time.

Banco Bilbao Vizcaya Argentaria (BBVA)

BBVA is a Spanish multinational financial services company, one of the largest financial institutes in the world. BBVA wants to optimise financial investment portfolios, which requires them to explore the best configuration of assets to maximise profit returns and minimise potential risks. The values of these assets are usually dynamic and affected by various factors, for example, transation costs. Classical techniques typically cannot calculate the optimal trading path considering all the associated varying factors. As a result, BBVA has started to experiment with quantum computing tools (BBVA, 2019).

Since 2019, BBVA has collaborated with multiple stakeholders to explore quantum computing, including Accenture, Multiverse (a Spanish quantum algorithm start-up), Zapata (a US quantum algorithms start-up), and Search Results (the Spanish National Research Council). The collaboration has resulted in several experiments in dynamic portfolio optimisation in a real financial context. One of their published papers in 2022 (Mugel et al., 2022) suggested that a quantum approach may ultimately outperform the equivalent classical approach, reducing the time taken from days to seconds.

Moody's

Moody's, a major global ratings agency, developed classical machine-learning algorithms to classify recessions, using national and global market data to forecast the risks of future recessions. These models predict the probability of a recession with a number of variables, including consumer (e.g., house prices), industrial (e.g., industry price index), and macro financial (e.g., stock prices, yield curves). The model specifications vary by country and are based on the timing and availability of data. Moody's worked with Rigetti Computing to increase the accuracy of forecasting economic recessions (Paini et al., 2023). The objective was to identify the inflection point at which quantum computers can solve a practical, operationally relevant problem with improved accuracy, speed or cost, compared to the best classical digital computers. Initial research using back-testing of recession data shows a potential improvement of around 5% in predicting recessions using the quantum approach compared to classical digital computers.

Quantum Machine Learning and Pattern Recognition

Quantum machine learning combines quantum mechanics and classical machine learning, with the aim of extracting meaningful information from complex data sets for pattern recognition. The problem domains in this application area include image classification, speech recognition, natural language processing, and object detection. Quantum methods may reduce cross-talk and enhance both the speed and accuracy of pattern recognition.

DSTL

The Defence Science and Technology Laboratory (DSTL) is an executive agency of the UK Ministry of Defence. It has purchased the UK government's first quantum computer, ORCA's PT-1 model, to be applied to complex machine learning and optimisation tasks (BBC, 2022). These include image analysis, handwriting recognition, and decision-making.

HSBC, Rigetti, and the Quantum Software Lab

HSBC, Rigetti, and the Quantum Software Lab are working on extending anomaly-detection quantum machine-learning models to detect anomalous behaviour that indicates money laundering (Rigetti, 2023). They expect quantum computing to enhance existing classical computing workflows, offering improved machine-learning methods.

Business, Economic, and Management Implications

As demonstrated in the above case studies, incumbent firms and organisations face a range of issues with classical digital computing. These issues include addressing optimisation and combinatorial problems, simulating dynamic systems, or recognising new patterns, all of which represent significant business challenges for many industries across the financial, pharmaceutical, transportation and mobility, and manufacturing sectors. As a result, start-ups are developing quantum computing hardware to address these issues using quantum mechanics and developing new algorithms to take advantage of the speed that quantum hardware may offer for certain problems. These niche innovations have led to the emergence and continuous updating of quantum computing technologies, with diverse competing variants in the market, forming and transforming the existing socio-technical regime. Innovations have also come from new established business partnerships and collaborations. Incumbent firms who expect to leverage quantum advantage are formulating new collaborations and value networks, with hardware providers, software firms, customers, universities, and governments, to co-explore and unlock the business value of quantum computing, helping to develop quantum computing and its emergence in the market.

Macro-level changes such as new policy initiatives and establishing government-led initiatives such as the UK's National Quantum Computing Centre provide funding and incentives for technological innovations using quantum computing. Multiple funding models from government are being used to stimulate investment in quantum, and policy support is being given to quantum computing projects, creating opportunities to stimulate the emergence and development of quantum computing start-ups. Consulting companies and system integrators are becoming crucial and instrumental to accelerating the value creation of quantum computing and its integration into the existing socio-technical regime. Drawing on a multi-level perspective, we can see that society is experiencing a dramatic quantum-enabled socio-technical transition—and the associated business value innovation.

Quantum computing is at an experimental stage of development, with firms learning from various trials being conducted. Most of these experiments are motivated by three key drivers, the first of which is firms having a business problem where there are opportunities to develop a better solution, including optimising logistics routing or simulating materials for next-generation battery technology.

The second driver is the need to address wider societal challenges. For example, the Novo Nordisk Foundation has pledged investment funds to build a quantum computer for the life sciences industry. This charitable foundation believes that quantum computing is a general-purpose technology that should be available to solve some of the grand challenges of society, such as healthcare. Funding by the foundation is based on the premise that quantum computing development by private-sector firms might lead to only addressing healthcare issues where there are profits to be made. Good health outcomes are a public good for society, which requires a non-profit organisation to contribute.

Finally, the third driver is the government acting as a buyer. This model is relatively common in the USA through agencies such as the Defense Advanced Research Agency (DARPA), which can provide guaranteed demand in the market, providing confidence of the proof of concept for the rest of the private sector to invest in the technology. For example, the UK's Ministry of Defence has acquired a quantum computer from ORCA Computing, a start-up firm developing full-stack photonic computing. In addition, through the funding agency Innovate UK, the UK government has provided funding through a catalyst fund to accelerate the adoption of quantum solutions in the public sector, covering projects ranging from optimising power grids to achieving net-zero targets. They are also developing the seven testbeds selected by the NQCC, where the UK government will act as the initial customer. Meanwhile, the German government has funded Universal Quantum to develop trapped ion computers for application in defence problems. And the Australian government has announced that it will invest nearly A$1 billion (funded by the federal government and Queensland state government) in the development of quantum computers by PsiQuantum, which is headquartered in the USA but was co-founded by a team including two Australian researchers. PsiQuantum will use the funds to build and operate its quantum computers in Brisbane, Australia, with a view to upgrading them in the future (*New Scientist*, 2024).

Incumbent firms often leverage the knowledge of a previous generation of technology where they have experience developing quantum computers. For example, IBM built on its experience in complementary metal oxide semiconductor (CMOS) technology to focus on developing superconducting qubits, which require cryogenic temperatures. However, the control and optical circuitry, which typically operates at room temperature, also needs to be incorporated into the cryogenic integrated chip architecture. New start-up firms often develop new technologies, such as ion traps or photonic computing, to create quantum computers. This is an example of Clayton Christensen's innovator dilemma, whereby incumbent firms typically focus on improving an existing technology to serve their customer needs, while new entrants initially tend to focus on niche markets (Christensen, 2015). It would be interesting to see whether quantum computing changes the dynamics of this tension—and how it plays out—to determine the dominant quantum computing design, and which firms might be future leaders.

Incumbent firms might also be willing to work with start-up firms to complement their capabilities, such as developing error-correction functionality, an important step in developing fault-tolerant machines following the current raft of noisy and error-prone intermediate-scale quantum computers (NISQ computers). Start-up firms such as Riverlane are developing error-correction middleware layers, with the aim of being hardware agnostic.

Moreover, there should be enough incentives to enable technology providers (e.g., photonic firms) to get more involved in quantum technologies. An absence of technological standards and a lack of systems integrators could affect the supply-side ecosystem development (Velu et al., 2022). The absence of a major systems integrator firm (such as IBM, Google, Microsoft) in the UK prompted the government to set up a National Quantum Computing Centre (NQCC) to act as a national initiative, and a proxy promoter of system-integration capabilities to build quantum computing capability in the UK. The NQCC recently selected seven firms to develop quantum computing testbeds (prototype quantum computers), helping to develop the UK's quantum infrastructure, accelerate quantum adoption in industry, and explore critical factors to improve quantum computing performance (NQCC, 2024;

Velu and Norman, 2025). These firms have different underlying hardware platforms (e.g., photonic, trapped ions, superconducting qubits, and cold atoms) and are setting up their hardware at the NQCC facilities. Examining the macro, meso, and micro dynamics across the multi-level perspective (MLP), together with the business model design, would give rise to several research questions.

Research has demonstrated that quantum computing offers profound transformative potential for existing businesses, management, and the economy. Reports from quantum computing stakeholders, including consulting firms such as McKinsey, technology user firms such as NVIDIA, and government sectors such as the US National Science and Technology Council, suggest that quantum computing will enable the development of a major value chain and market demand. Significant investment will be required to initiate its development and adoption (Hazan et al., 2020; NASEM 2019; NVIDIA, 2023).

However, the business applications and use cases that will generate business value remain uncertain, which is the main challenge at the current stage of quantum computing commercialisation. Efforts have been made to identify potential quantum computing business applications (e.g., McKinsey, 2021). The promising returns from business value generated from quantum computing in the future, and uncertain business applications of quantum computing currently, create windows of opportunity for researching quantum computing in many areas of management and business research.

In information systems research, opportunities are emerging such as the initiative of national programmes that could nurture dedicated quantum computing resources and support, cloud-based services that could create more accessibility from different stakeholder levels, and integration with AI or other application areas that could generate more implementation and operational change (Egger et al., 2020; Rietsche et al., 2022; Ur Rasool et al., 2023).

Yet, challenges arising from quantum computing remain, in the domain of cyber-security, national security, quantum education and workforce development, and sustainable quantum ecosystems. For example, the risk that quantum computing poses to existing encryption techniques in cyber-security could result in confidential and sensitive data being leaked if organisations fail to understand the impact of quantum on their existing digital system (Faruk et al. 2022). This indicates the potential of political change, such as providing quantum computing education at an individual level, senior management committing to quantum adoption at organisational level, or developing scale-up guidelines and ethical regulations for quantum computing at industrial and country levels. Kar et al. (2024) have indicated the importance of incorporating quantum computing in Information Systems (IS) research and other salient research areas, such as the impact of quantum computing on industry and society, quantum education and workforce development, quantum governance and regulations, and the adoption of quantum computing systems. Promising IS theoretical foundations could be employed, including network economics, information flow efficiencies, technology access, technology embeddedness, computational capabilities, and the nature of digital transformation.

In business research, quantum computing has demonstrated a strong potential for firms to maintain competitive advantage. Quantum computing has demonstrated promising business value for firms, even though quantum business applications remain challenging. Ruane et al. (2022) divided potential quantum computing business applications into five categories: (1) simulating chemical interactions, reactors of clean technology, and materials such as batteries or cells; (2) linear systems for enhanced machine learning/AI and large data transfers; (3) optimising investment portfolios, supply chain routes, and manufacturing facilities; (4) unstructured searches from large amounts of data with faster speed and improved accuracy; and (5) factoring and encrypting existing security and privacy. However, the adequacy of these classifications remains unknown. Bova et al. (2021) argue that the most important domain for quantum computing to address is a combinatorial problem: how objects can be better combined. They propose three potential combinatorial applications, including quantum-safe encryption on classical computers, material and drug discovery, and quantum-inspired algorithms for classical computers. This indicates that characterising quantum problem domains is worthy of scrutiny in quantum computing business research.

Furthermore, the issue for firms of how to secure competitive advantage in quantum computing business leadership remains challenging. Business managers considering quantum computing are facing a business dilemma and encountering a difficult trade-off: investing early in quantum computing and being a first mover could result in significant risks with few benefits before quantum computing becomes mature; and delaying investment could result in giving away competitive advantage to the early risk takers (Sodhi & Tayur, 2022). Therefore, securing the competitive advantage created by quantum computing, while maintaining a low-risk profile from the unknown return on investment, is a challenge that is worth investigating. Ruane et al. (2022) suggest that managers need: (1) vigilance when it comes to quantum computing's technological development; and (2) a vision for planning quantum computing application scenarios, and an understanding of the potential impact of quantum on their current business. Whether these are sufficient remains unknown.

Sodhi and Tayur (2022) suggest three strategies that firms should use to address the quantum computing business dilemma. First, managers should consider identifying the business applications of quantum computing rather than hesitating about quantum technical maturity and readiness. Second, firms should understand how quantum computing can benefit their business, and their real needs going forwards, in order to leverage quantum computing capabilities as soon as they are ready. And, third, they should invest in quantum-inspired computing using classical computers before quantum computing becomes a reality, as firms can leverage quantum-inspired computing to test the benefits in advance, mitigating the risk from fully investing in real quantum computers now. However, these approaches are still inadequate for firms to fully address the business issue of quantum computing. For example, quantum-inspired computing cannot leverage all of the benefits of quantum mechanics; thus, it cannot sufficiently address the business problems with quantum advantage, which could pose risks for other entrant firms investing in real quantum computing. Therefore, research is needed to fully understand the value chain of quantum computing in business and industry.

In management and organisation research, adopting and implementing quantum computing could raise various concerns and changes in organisations. Introducing quantum computing to organisations may require not just sufficient technical maturity but also a clear positioning in the current organisational ecosystem. Bhasin and Tripathi (2021) argue that quantum computing needs to be gradually embedded and integrated into existing legacy systems to work seamlessly with classical computing. Adopting quantum computing in organisations could be inhibited by factors such as the absence of a business strategy around quantum computing, a lack of co-creation ecosystems, quantum computing acquisition cultures, support from the organisational structure, high sustainability and development costs, a shortage of quantum skills and training programmes, continued financial availability, high technological risk, a shortage of IT interoperability, and uncertain regulations. Besides, organisations generally face significant uncertainties, equivocality, and tensions in their structure, which needs to be addressed as quantum computing is introduced. For example, in healthcare organisations, quantum computing is expected to advance current healthcare techniques to generate more precise and timely solutions to patient problems, resulting in a disruptive impact on healthcare organisation structures and reflecting a change in their information-processing needs (Gupta et al., 2023). These organisational implications inform some salient research questions in understanding and managing quantum computing in organisations. Properly understanding and managing the adoption and impact of quantum technologies in organisations, the associated organisational structure and flows, the enablers and inhibitors for quantum computing adoption, and the mitigation strategy around tensions, require further study in management and organisation research.

Summary of Business Implications and Potential Research Questions

In this chapter, we examined how new quantum computing businesses are coming to market (the micro level in the multi-level perspective), in some cases building partnerships with incumbent firms (the meso level). We also considered the role of government (the macro level) in creating initiatives to develop the quantum ecosystem, for example, by acting as a direct customer of these emerging technologies. It would be interesting to explore what else could take place at the macro level to enhance these technologies in the market. For example, how could governments introduce societal grand challenges around quantum computing to incentivise scale-up? What form should such grand challenges take? And what should the "institutional logic" be at the macro level? For example, what institutions are needed in government to monitor and encourage an emerging ecosystem? And what facilities should they provide (e.g., national labs or user facilities)? What regulatory frameworks might be required?

We touched on Christensen's innovator dilemma. Given that the emerging quantum computing ecosystem could be viewed as a "living lab", it would be interesting to examine the response of incumbent firms to new entrants through this lens. How radical should incumbents' responses be to quantum technologies? How quickly should they respond? And how should they organise internally? There are also questions of learning, cognition, and "framing" in this context. For example, how should incumbents describe quantum computing, internally and to their customers? And how would this framing lead to revising the understanding of the value of quantum technologies to incumbent firms and their customers? How would this impact their business models? And their customers' business models and organisational structures?

At the micro level, we explored in this chapter a variety of hardware modalities for quantum computing and looked at some business applications that customers are exploring. Given this wide range of applications and hardware combinations, how should new entrants decide on their business approach (e.g., full-stack versus hardware components, or niche application expertise versus breadth)? Is quantum computing "special" in this context? For example, compared to classical computing, how long will it take for hardware and software applications to come together? How should new entrants engage with potential customers to define the potential value of their offerings? And how should they leverage the power of incumbent firms (e.g., by providing access to new products as a service using an existing incumbent's infrastructure)? We summarise these questions in Table 2.2.

Quantum computing promises increased computational capabilities, with the capacity to solve a wide range of problems, with major transformative opportunities to address societies' grand challenges in healthcare, climate change, and other areas.

Table 2.2 Potential research questions around quantum computing

Level	*Sub-Question*
Macro level	• How could governments introduce societal grand challenges to incentivise private firms to scale up? • How could the institutional logic be changed as quantum computing is introduced? • How could quantum computing regulations or related policy be developed?
Meso level—in general	• How do incumbent firms already in the DC market build capabilities in quantum computing? What are the ways to overcome inertia? • What impact does quantum computing have on organising and innovation practices as it is adopted and implemented in incumbent firms? • What types of business or management problem could be solved by quantum computing? How are these applications identified, developed, and addressed? • What roles or stakeholders should be involved in developing quantum applications? What collaboration modes, ecosystems, or practices should be developed to advance quantum computing commercialisation?
Meso level—in the specifics of business models	• How does one determine the value of quantum computing? How could quantum computing be cognitively framed, and how should societal value be created/captured? How does the value network emerge and develop over time? • Is it worth companies investing now?
Micro level	• How do start-up firms decide whether to build full-stack or specific niche areas (hardware, software, and so on)? • What is the best approach to work with incumbents?

References

Airbus. (2024). *Is quantum computing an enabler for the decarbonisation of aviation?* https://www.airbus.com/en/newsroom/stories/2024-04-is-quantum-computing-an-enabler-for-the-decarbonisation-of-aviation

Auffèves, A. (2022). Quantum technologies need a quantum Energy initiative. *PRX Quantum, 3*, Article 020101.

BBC. (2022). *Ministry of Defence acquires government's first quantum computer*. https://www.bbc.co.uk/news/technology-61647134

BBVA. (2019). *BBVA and CSIC research the potential of quantum computing in the financial sector*. https://www.bbva.com/en/bbva-and-csic-research-the-potential-of-quantum-computing-in-the-financial-sector/

Bhasin, A., & Tripathi, M. (2021). Quantum computing at an inflection point: Are we ready for a new paradigm. *IEEE Transactions on Engineering Management, 70*(7), 2546–2557.

Bosch. (2022). *Quantum technologies push the boundaries of what is possible*. https://www.bosch.com/research/research-fields/digitalization-and-connectivity/research-on-quantum-technologies/

Bova, F. et al. (2021). Commercial applications of quantum computing. *EPJ Quantum Technology*, *8*(2).

Bromley, A. G. (1982, July–September). Charles Babbage's Analytical Engine, 1838. *IEEE Annals of the History of Computing*, *4*(3), 197–217.

Brynjolfsson, E., & Hitt, L. M. (2003). Computing Productivity: Firm-Level Evidence. *The Review of Economics and Statistics, 85*(4), 793–808.

Cazzola, P., & Lassman, J. (2021). Decarbonising Air Transport: Acting Now for the Future. *International Transport Forum Policy Papers, 94*. OECD Publishing, Paris.

Christensen, C. (2015). *The innovator's Dilemma: When new technologies cause great firms to fail*. Harvard Business Review Press.

Cortada, J. W. (2004). *The digital hand: How computers changed the work of American manufacturing, transportation, and retail industries*. Oxford University Press.

Courtland, R. (2015). The law that's not a law. *IEEE Spectrum, 52*(4).

Delgado, A., Casares, P. A., Dos Reis, R., Zini, M. S., Campos, R., Cruz-Hernández, N., & Arrazola, J. M. (2022). Simulating key properties of lithium-ion batteries with a fault-tolerant quantum computer. *Physical Review A, 106*(3), Article 032428.

Deutsch, D., & Jozsa, R. (1992). Rapid solutions of problems by quantum computation. *Proceedings of the Royal Society of London a., 439*(1907), 553–558.

Economou, S., Rudoph, T., & Barnes, E. (2020). Teaching quantum information science to high-school and early undergraduate students. arXiv:2005.07874.

Egger, D. J., Gambella, C., Marecek, J., McFaddin, S., Mevissen, M., Raymond, R., & Yndurain, E. (2020). Quantum computing for finance: State-of-the-art and future prospects. *IEEE Transactions on Quantum Engineering, 1*, 1–24.
Faruk, M. J. H., Tahora, S., Tasnim, M., Shahriar, H., & Sakib, N. (May 2022). A review of quantum cybersecurity: threats, risks and opportunities. In *2022 1st International Conference on AI in Cybersecurity (ICAIC)* (pp. 1–8). IEEE.
Feynman, R. (1982). Simulating physics with computers. *International Journal of Theoretical Physics, 21*(6/7), 467–488.
Frank, L. (2022). *The story of LEO—The World's first business computer.* Warwick University—Modern Records Centre. https://warwick.ac.uk/services/library/mrc/archives_online/digital/leo/story
Gupta, S., Modgil, S., Bhatt, P. C., Jabbour, C. J. C., & Kamble, S. (2023). Quantum computing led innovation for achieving a more sustainable Covid-19 healthcare industry. *Technovation, 120*, Article 102544.
Hazan, E., Ménard, A., Ostojic, I., & Patel, M. (2020). *The next tech revolution: quantum computing*. McKinsey & Company. https://www.mckinsey.com/fr/~/media/McKinsey/Locations/Europe%20and%20Middle%20East/France/Our%20Insights/The%20next%20tech%20revolution%20Quantum%20Computing/Quantum-Computing.ashx
IBM. (2022). *Bosch partnering with IBM on strategic quantum computing materials science engagement*. https://newsroom.ibm.com/2022-11-09-Bosch-Partnering-with-IBM-on-Strategic-Quantum-Computing-Materials-Science-Engagement
IoTWorldToday. (2023). *Nvidia, Rolls-Royce, Classiq Tap Quantum for Jet Engine Design*. https://www.iotworldtoday.com/transportation-logistics/nvidia-rolls-royce-classiq-tap-quantum-for-jet-engine-design
Kalai, G. (2016). The quantum computer puzzle. *Notices of the American Mathematical Society, 63*(5), 508–516.
Kar, A. K., He, W., Payton, F. C., Grover, V., Al-Busaidi, A. S., & Dwivedi, Y. K. (2024). How could quantum computing shape information systems research–An editorial perspective and future research directions. *International Journal of Information Management*, 102776.
McKinsey. (2021). *Quantum computing use cases are getting real—What you need to know*. https://www.mckinsey.com/capabilities/mckinsey-digital/our-insights/quantum-computing-use-cases-are-getting-real-what-you-need-to-know
Mugel, S., Kuchkovsky, C., Sanchez, E., Fernandez-Lorenzo, S., Luis-Hita, J., Lizaso, E., & Orus, R. (2022). Dynamic portfolio optimization with real datasets using quantum processors and quantum-inspired tensor networks. *Physical Review Research, 4*(1), Article 013006.
National Academies of Sciences, Engineering, and Medicine (NASEM). (2019). *Quantum computing: Progress and prospects.* The National Academies Press.

New Scientist. (2024, April 30). Australia places A$1 billion bet on quantum computing firm PsiQuantum.

NQCC. (2023). NQCC, Rolls-Royce and Riverlane partner to accelerate materials discovery. https://www.nqcc.ac.uk/updates/nqcc-rolls-royce-and-riverlane-partner-to-accelerate-materials-discovery/

NQCC. (2024). Science Minister Andrew Griffith announces the results of the £30m quantum computing testbed competition, www.nqcc.ac.uk

NVIDIA. (2023). NVIDIA, Rolls-Royce and Classiq Announce Quantum Computing Breakthrough for Computational Fluid Dynamics in Jet Engines. https://nvidianews.nvidia.com/news/nvidia-rolls-royce-and-classiq-announce-quantum-computing-breakthrough-for-computational-fluid-dynamics-in-jet-engines

OurWorldInData.org/technological-change. (2022). https://ourworldindata.org/grapher/transistors-per-microprocessor

Paini et al. (2023). Recession Prediction via Signature Kernels Enhanced with Quantum Features | by Rigetti Computing | Rigetti | Medium.

Paudel, H. P., Syamlal, M., Crawford, S. E., Lee, Y.-L., Shugayev, R. A., Lu, P., & Duan, Y. (2022). Quantum computing and simulation for energy applications: Review and perspective. *ACS Engineering Au, 2*(3), 151–196.

Peruzzo, A. et al. (2014, July 23). A variational eigenvalue solver on a photonic quantum processor. *Nature Communications* (5), 4213.

Pharmaphorum. (2017). Biogen go quantum to speed up drug development.gup, https://pharmaphorum.com/news/biogen-quantum-drug-development

Preskill, J. (2018). Quantum computing in the NISQ era and beyond. *Quantum, 2*, 79.

Proctor, T. et al. (2024). Benchmarking quantum computers. arXiv:2407.08828.

Quantum Algorithm Zoo. (2024). https://quantumalgorithmzoo.org/

Rietsche, R., Dremel, C., Bosch, S., Steinacker, L., Meckel, M., & Leimeister, J. M. (2022). Quantum computing. *Electronic Markets, 32*(4), 2525–2536.

Rigetti. (2023). Rigetti computing awarded innovate UK grant to enhance quantum machine learning methods for anti-money laundering detection, https://www.globenewswire.com/news-release/2023/11/01/2771203/0/en/Rigetti-Computing-Awarded-Innovate-UK-Grant-to-Enhance-Quantum-Machine-Learning-Methods-for-Anti-Money-Laundering-Detection.html

Ruane, J. et al. (2022, January–February). Quantum Computing for Business Leaders. *Harvard Business Review*, 112–121.

Shannon, C. (1948). A mathematical theory of communication. *The Bell System Technical Journal, 27*(379–423), 623–656.

Sodhi, M. S., & Tayur, S. R. (2022). Make your business quantum-ready today. *Management and Business Review, 2*(2), 78–84.

Ur Rasool, R., Ahmad, H. F., Rafique, W., Qayyum, A., Qadir, J., & Anwar, Z. (2023). Quantum computing for healthcare: A review. *Future Internet, 15*(3), 94.

Velu, C., Putra, F., Geurtsen, E., Norman, K., & Noble, C. (2022). *Adoption of Quantum Technologies and Business Model Innovation*. Institute for Manufacturing, University of Cambridge.

Velu, C., & Putra, F. (2023). How to introduce quantum computers without slowing economic growth. *Nature, 619*(7970), 461–464.

Velu, C., & Norman, K. (2025). *NQCC Quantum Testbed Pilot Study*. Institute for Manufacturing, University of Cambridge. https://www.ifm.eng.cam.ac.uk/uploads/News/NQCC_Quantum_Computing_Testbed_Pilot_Study_Oct_2025.pdf

Volkswagen. (2022). https://www.volkswagen-group.com/en/press-releases/volkswagen-group-and-xanadu-establish-quantum-simulation-program-for-battery-materials-16561

Wannakrairoj, W., & Velu, C. (February 2021). Productivity growth and business model innovation. *Economics Letters, 199*, Article 109679.

CHAPTER 3

Quantum Communications and Enhancing Security

This chapter covers:

- *How the security of our communication systems uses cryptographic methods that rely on mathematical complexity (i.e. the difficulty of finding the prime factors of a large number), and why this is a weakness for Quantum 2.0 technologies?*
- *What are the alternative solutions:*
  - *post-quantum cryptography (PQC)?*
  - *quantum key distribution (QKD)?*
- *An outline of how PQC and QKD can be complementary, and what governments and firms are doing to provide enhanced security;*
- *Some initial deployment of QKD systems and PQC solutions;*
- *Applications and developments in deploying satellites;*
- *Developments in the quantum-enabled internet;*
- *A discussion of the possible business and economic implications using the frameworks outlined in Chapter 1;*
- *An outline of research questions to be explored further.*

C. Velu et al., *The Business of Quantum Technologies*,
https://doi.org/10.1007/978-3-031-99808-9_3

Introduction

This chapter explores applying quantum mechanics to keep data safe. Data security has always been a prime concern of defence organisations, but with the development of the internet in the 1990s, the need to keep data secure has risen sharply. We have become used to using passwords and fingerprint and face scanners to secure our financial transactions and medical records; and, increasingly, online messaging services have introduced end-to-end encryption to ensure that our data are only accessible to those with the correct level of access. In this chapter, we will explore some of the issues with classical encryption and discuss how quantum mechanics allows us to encrypt data more securely than ever before. We also discuss developments in quantum networks and the quantum-enabled internet.

Classical Encryption

Let us recall from the previous chapter where we described how a sequence of classical bits can be used to encode information—we used the examples that 01000111 might represent the character "G" in a text document, and the sequence 000000001111111100000000 might represent the colour green in an image file. The principle that a sequence of bits can represent an item of data is quite generic, essentially applying to any sort of information. All that is required is an agreed encryption/decryption key, which maps the original information onto the sequence of bits. In the simplest case, the data to be encrypted are compared with an agreed mapping and decrypted by reversing the mapping operation. For example, to encode the message "HELLO WORLD", the sender of the message looks up the key mapping for each letter to generate an encoded string and then transmits that string. The receiver looks up each element of the string against the reversed mapping to regenerate the message (see Fig. 3.1).

This simple scheme is commonly used in classical computing and is analogous to ciphers like Morse code, where every letter has a mapping to a simple sequence (in the case of Morse code, dots and dashes rather than 0s and 1s). Conceptually, it relies on both parties knowing the mapping between the plain text of the original message and the encrypted text. Crucially, the *same* key is used for *both* encryption and decryption—the decryption operation is simply the reverse of the encryption operation.

Message : HELLO WORLD

Letter	Bit sequence	Letter	Bit Sequence
A	01000001	...	...
B	01000010	O	01001111
C	01000011	...	...
D	01000100	R	01010010
E	01000101	...	...
...	...	W	01010111
H	01001000	X	01011000
....	...	Y	01011001
L	01001100	Z	01011010

Encrypted message : 01001000 01000101 01001100 01001100 01001111 01010111 01001111 01010010 01001100 01000100

Letter	Bit sequence	Letter	Bit Sequence
A	01000001	...	...
B	01000010	O	01001111
C	01000011	...	...
D	01000100	R	01010010
E	01000101	...	...
...	...	W	01010111
H	01001000	X	01011000
....	...	Y	01011001
L	01001100	Z	01011010

Decrypted message : HELLO WORLD

Fig. 3.1 A simple encoding scheme

Practically, for simple cases like this, it is possible to guess the key, particularly if the original message is long enough. More sophisticated mappings can make it harder to guess the original message, but both sender and receiver must agree on the specific key they will use—thus, they should exchange the agreed mapping algorithm. For this reason, this method of encryption is always vulnerable to attack: even if a third party cannot guess the mapping algorithm used in a particular message, they can potentially still intercept the exchange of the key or mapping algorithm between sender and receiver. If the third party is careful, they may be able to intercept the exchange of mapping without anybody else knowing (e.g., by taking a copy of the mapping).

How, then, is data kept safe on digital systems and the internet? Modern internet encryption relies on more sophisticated techniques. The sender and receiver still agree on mappings, but instead of using one mapping that encrypts and decrypts, *the sender encrypts with one mapping and the receiver decrypts with a different one*. Think about this carefully—there are now two keys, one used to encrypt and a different one used to decrypt. At first glance, this looks impossible; it is like a door that is locked with one key but can only be unlocked with a different key. However, such keys do exist in some mathematical operations, called one-way functions. These can be viewed as mathematical problems that are easy to solve in one direction but very hard to solve in another.

For example, given two large prime numbers, it is easy to multiply them together—you may need a calculator, but in principle it is straightforward. However, given only the answer to that calculation, it is generally hard to determine the original two numbers. For instance, if you were asked to find two numbers that multiply together to make the number 21 (other than 1 and 21), you would easily see that the numbers are 3 and 7. However, what two numbers when multiplied together make 12,827 (other than 1 and 12,827)? Even with a calculator, this is a harder problem—few obvious shortcuts significantly improve the "brute-force" approach of simply trying every combination of numbers starting from 1. Nevertheless, if you were asked to multiply 101 by 127, it would only take a few moments to find that $101 \times 127 = 12{,}827$. The calculation in one direction is very easy, but in the other direction, it is much harder.

Given a classical digital computer, this example is not particularly hard, but if the computer were programmed to find the two prime numbers that multiply together to make, say, 26,987,476,709,771, the problem becomes moderately difficult (the correct answer is 15,485,863

× 1,742,717). For typical internet security, the numbers used have hundreds of digits. Using even the most powerful classical computers, finding the prime factors of such large numbers is practically impossible, with current estimates suggesting it would take trillions of years to perform this calculation.

We now begin to see how to build an algorithm that encrypts data with one key but decrypts it with a different one. Each party keeps two large prime numbers and uses each number to generate a key, such that each party has a *public key* and a *private key*. These keys are related by mathematical operations similar to those described above. The public keys are shared freely with anyone who wants to send that party a message. The sender uses the recipient's public key to encrypt the message, like using a key that locks a door. However, at this point, even the sender of the message cannot decrypt that message. The *public* key of the recipient has *locked* it but crucially is *not able to unlock* it. The recipient uses their *private* key to decrypt the message. The method has locked the door with one key but unlocked it with a different one, which only the recipient possesses.

Quantum Decryption

We have seen how data can be kept secure from classical computing power by relying on the complexity of certain calculations that are easy for a classical computer to do in one direction but much harder to do in a different one. Variations on this method are used in standard internet security protocols, and until the mid-1990s, it was thought this was practically unbreakable. In reality, there is always a very small chance in these encryption techniques of "getting lucky" and guessing the correct private keys, similar to trying every possible key in a physical lock until you find the right one—not impossible but extremely unlikely using a classical computer.

Then, in 1994, Peter Shor at AT&T Bell Labs described how a quantum computer that was large enough could factor a large prime number exponentially faster than classical methods could (Shor, 1994; see also discussion in Chapter 2). The method involves "guessing" a number and defining a particular mathematical relationship between this number and the original large number; and, using the quantum computer's ability to utilise quantum superposition, examining this function to find a relationship between the target number and its factors.

This means Shor's algorithm can factor large numbers in significantly fewer steps than any known classical algorithm. How many fewer steps? Mathematically, Shor's algorithm offers an exponential speed-up over classical methods, meaning its runtime effectively scales as the logarithm of the number of digits in the original number. For factoring practical-sized numbers used in internet security, this is still likely to require the order of millions of qubits, with long lifetimes, and high fault tolerance. At that scale, typical internet security could be broken in a matter of days or hours. Quantum machines at this level are not currently available, but they could be realisable within a few years.

Nonetheless, even now, there are potential breaches of secure data. In principle, a rogue actor could steal encrypted data and wait until quantum machines are available to decrypt it. Some data retains its value—hence the need to keep it secure, for decades—so the challenges of "harvest now, decrypt later" should be taken seriously. Mosca and Paini (2023) describe three parameters that organisations should consider in light of quantum attacks:

- $T_{SHELF\text{-}LIFE}$ (shelf-life time): the number of years the information should be protected by the cyber-system.
- $T_{MIGRATION}$ (migration time): the number of years needed to migrate the system properly and safely to a quantum-safe solution.
- T_{THREAT} (threat timeline): the number of years before the relevant threat actors will be able to break the quantum-vulnerable systems.

If $T_{SHELF\text{-}LIFE} + T_{MIGRATION} > T_{THREAT}$, an organisation may not be able to protect its data for the required $T_{SHELF\text{-}LIFE}$ years against the quantum threat. Mosca and Paini also estimate that there is a realistic possibility of a sufficiently powerful quantum machine being developed before the end of the decade. Organisations should not underestimate the effort involved in transferring their data assets to quantum-safe solutions once they have become standardised.

Does any of this mean internet security is on the verge of being broken? The simple answer is a "cautious no". Over the last two decades, the mathematics and computer science community has developed quantum-resistant algorithms, often described as post-quantum cryptography (PQC). This is an evolving field, but it should offer long-term security against both classical and quantum attacks. Researchers are investigating several approaches (e.g., Bernstein, 2009), and the UK National Cyber Security Centre (NCSC) anticipates that some approaches will be more suited to particular applications than others (NCSC, 2020). The US National Institute of Standards and Technology (NIST) has been running a research programme on quantum-resistant algorithms (NIST, 2016) and evaluated several dozen proposed techniques; the institute announced its down selection of three post-quantum encryption methods in 2024 (NIST, 2024). The White House began providing all federal agencies with instructions on migrating to post-quantum cryptography in 2022 (NSM-10, 2022), and NIST published draft Federal Information Processing Standards for Post Quantum Cryptography for comment in 2023. Other international bodies, such as the European Telecommunications Standards Institute (ETSI), are also actively engaged in post-quantum cryptography standardisation (ETSI, 2020). Data communication companies will need to implement these standards, but for the "average customer" the impact on the user experience will remain largely unchanged.

In parallel, a further technique is being developed that, rather than the mathematical techniques being tested for PQC, relies on physics to ensure data has not been tampered with. This method is referred to as quantum key distribution (QKD). There are several variations of QKD, based on the properties of entangled photons, or on how the parties choose to measure the states of the photons. In all cases, if a rogue actor attempts to listen in on the communication, the state of the photons is inevitably disturbed. With suitable agreements between sender and receiver, any such attempt to "listen in" on the message will be detected (see Box 3.1).

In principle, this means that QKD provides untappable security. In practice, there are many technical challenges to overcome before QKD gains acceptance. In particular, it does not offer a native way to authenticate the communicating parties, meaning they must use alternative methods (potentially classical encryption methods) to ensure they are who they say they are.

That said, several commercial QKD networks are already available, and in the UK, BT and Toshiba provide access to a metro QKD network as a pilot study that has been tested by major firms such as EY (2022) and HSBC (2023). There is also potential for utilising QKD in free space (i.e. without cabling infrastructure), and using QKD via orbiting satellites may be important for long-distance commercial quantum-resistant communication networks.

Box 3.1 A QKD Primer There are several different implementations of quantum key distribution (QKD), but in general, all implementations rely on how quantum mechanical objects called photons are measured. Photons are quantum packets of light waves. The electric field component associated with a light wave can be made to oscillate exclusively up and down compared to the overall direction of motion of the wave (vertical polarisation), or left and right compared to the direction of the wave (horizontal polarisation), or at some other angle. This principle carries over into the quantum mechanical description of light waves, in that photons can also be described as vertically or horizontally polarised. Because photons are quantum mechanical objects, they can also exist in a superposition of *both* horizontal and vertical polarisations. This is like our spinning coin analogy from Chapter 1, where a tossed coin spinning in the air can be described as simultaneously being in a superposition of a "heads state" and a "tails state". As for our spinning coin, when we measure the polarisation of a photon, we never observe it in a superposition; the act of measurement forces the photon into a definite polarisation state, just as catching a spinning coin on the back of our hands forces it into a definite heads or tails state.

To stretch our coin analogy, there are other ways we could catch a coin while it is spinning in the air. Instead of catching it horizontally, we could clap our hands vertically around it and observe its edge. We can do something similar with photons, in that we can measure their polarisation along a particular axis, be it horizontal, vertical, or some other angle. This is called choosing the basis of the measurement. However, our coin analogy now starts to break down. By measuring the polarisation of a photon along a different axis, we do not see the "edge" of the photon in the same way as we see the edge of a coin; rather, we always observe some definite polarisation state along that axis. It is this quantum mechanical property of photons that allows us to construct a method of privately sharing an encryption key.

To see how this works, consider Alice, who wishes to send an encrypted message to Bob. Alice pre-selects random measurement bases, corresponding to measuring photon polarisations horizontally (H) or vertically (V) (or $+ 45°$ (diagonal, D) or $-45°$ (antidiagonal, A)). She generates a string of photons, encoding a bitstring of 0s and 1s, with 0 encoded as H polarised and 1 as V polarised. She sends these measured photons to Bob, who also chooses a random set of measurement bases and measures the photons he receives using these bases. Alice and Bob can now share the details of the measurement bases they have each chosen, but crucially, they do *not* share the outcomes of their individual measurements. They can then individually, and secretly, compare their measurement results against the shared measurement bases.

If Alice and Bob's individual choices of measurement bases are truly random, 50% of the time they will not match. The bits associated with those "misses" are discarded. Where the measurement bases match, Alice and Bob are each guaranteed to observe the same polarisation (in practical implementations, allowances must be made to account for noise). These matching "hits" are used to generate a quantum encryption key. Both Alice and Bob end up with the same encryption key, despite never having communicated this key directly to each other. Figure 3.2 shows the generation of just two digits of an encryption key, but in practical implementations, longer keys are generated.

What if an eavesdropper attempts to intercept a message encoded with this key? Alice and Bob can publicly compare a portion of their generated keys. If an eavesdropper has intercepted the key distribution, the eavesdropper's measurement of the photon polarisations will have introduced errors into the bitstream, meaning Alice and Bob will know eavesdropping has taken place.

This example is a simplified explanation of the earliest description of QKD, based on the superposition of quantum states and referred to as the BB84 protocol (Bennett & Brassard, 1984). Other QKD protocols have since been developed based on quantum entanglement, for example, the E91 protocol (Ekert, 1991).

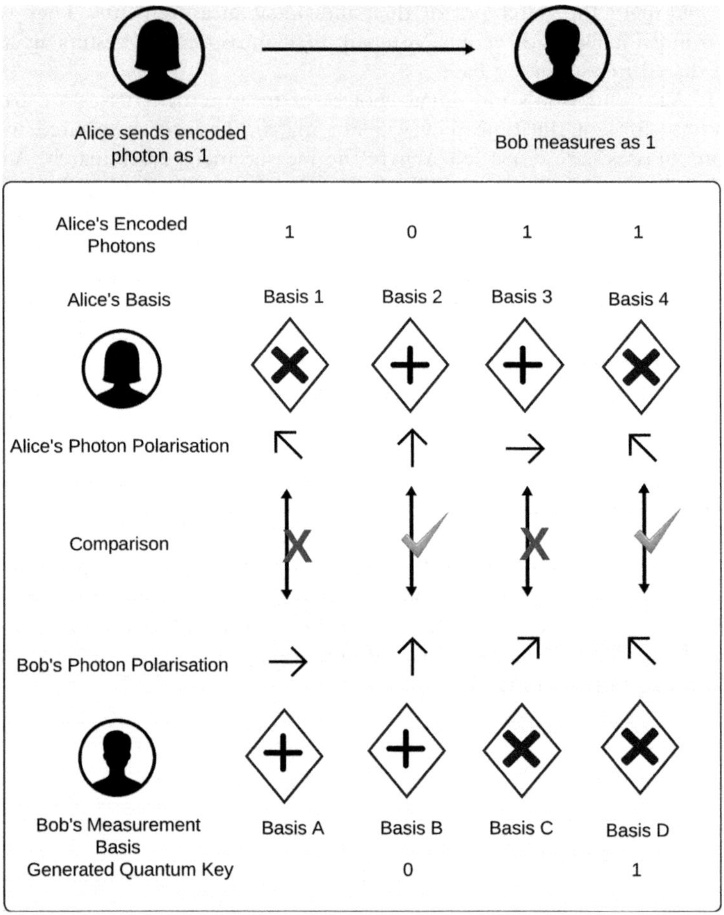

Fig. 3.2 Quantum key generation example (adapted from Haitjema, 2007)

A Quantum Internet?

When the practicality of encrypting data using quantum techniques has been fully industrialised, will we be able to build a "quantum internet"? In this context, we should distinguish between networks that specifically connect quantum processors, and long-range communications based on quantum superposition and entanglement, which may or may not involve quantum processors. Quantum processor networks exist, but there is currently no infrastructure that will connect two quantum processors separated by a significant distance (e.g., outside the lab). However, there are several examples of long-range QKD networks such as the BT–Toshiba collaboration in the UK, in Japan (Sasaki et al., 2011), Switzerland (Stucki et al., 2011), China (Chen et al., 2021), and elsewhere. In principle, these could connect quantum processors together, but equally they can be used to encrypt purely classical data—and it is in the latter sense that they are typically being deployed. Moreover, research has shown there are team decision problems where direct communication is not possible, but coordination among team members can be realised via quantum entangled signals in a shared environment, which could significantly improve performance compared to classical communication (Brandenburger & La Mura, 2016).

What needs to be done to build resilient technologies that will support reliable, quantum-based communications over long distances? There are several outstanding challenges. First, the "backbone" channel technology requires improvements. Maintaining quantum states in optical fibre over long distances is difficult, as is robust over-the-air transmission. Developing ***quantum repeaters*** is therefore important. In classical telecommunications, as the signal degrades over distance, a simple amplifier can be used to boost the signal. However, in quantum communications an amplifier would inevitably have to measure the qubits, thereby destroying a superposition. Instead, a true quantum repeater would enable entanglement of qubits over long distances without needing to send entangled qubits very far. A quantum repeater would receive an entangled qubit from one section of the network and entangle it with new qubits to send on to the next section of the network—known as quantum teleportation (Wehner et al., 2018). Quantum repeaters are being developed but are not yet commercially available. However, depending on the application, a true quantum internet may only need to maintain the information associated with a relatively small number of qubits, particularly if the goal is to use quantum entanglement to communicate a series of classical bits (as in QKD). In these cases, established classical error-correction techniques may be applied to the classical data before it is encoded. In the case of connecting quantum processors together, significant research is underway establishing lab-scale networks, enabling connectivity between quantum processors separated by a few metres, for example, in a server-room environment.

Notably, work is being carried out on *blind quantum computing* (Barz et al., 2012; Drmota 2024). This technique allows a client to perform calculations on a quantum server while keeping the computation private, including the details of the problem they are working on, the algorithm being used, and the output of the calculation. Compare this to classical computing, where a rogue actor could examine (and decrypt) the contents of a classical server to reverse-engineer what calculations it was performing. Blind quantum computing is likely to be important in developing true cloud-based quantum computing. A potential application of blind quantum computing enabled by the quantum internet may be the ability to securely share data and processing between firms. For example, it may be possible to implement distributed 3D printing, whereby learning from one firm's machines can be transferred to another without exposing the underlying data. This could result in sharing models for 3D printers globally, with new local-production-based business models emerging, contributing to a more sustainable economy (Velu & Putra, 2023). In addition, new emerging areas such as quantum currencies could underpin developments in blockchain and related technologies to provide a more secure financial system. Recalling that measuring a general quantum state necessarily destroys any superposition for that state (remember that "measuring" a flipped coin, we only ever find it to be either heads or tails, never a superposition of both) provides an intriguing way to potentially counter fraud. If the serial number on a banknote could be represented by a general quantum state, "reading" the serial number will necessarily destroy its quantum information, rendering it uncopiable. Effectively, this is an application of the so-called quantum no-cloning theorem, which states that it is impossible to reliably copy a general quantum state—in this case, applied in a way that makes it impossible to copy a serial number on a banknote.

Business Case Studies

In this section, we review the preliminary use cases in quantum communications.

BT and Toshiba

In April 2022, BT (a British multinational telecommunications company), Toshiba (a Japanese multinational electronics company), and EY (a multinational professional services firm) launched a pilot trial of QKD in London (BT Newsroom, 2022). It was the world's first commercial quantum-secured metro network, enabling EY to securely transmit valuable data and information between multiple offices over standard fibre-optic links using QKD. BT provided the high-bandwidth end-to-end encrypted links via a private fibre network, and Toshiba provided the key distribution hardware and key management software. In 2023, HSBC (a global bank) joined the QKD pilot together with Amazon Web Services (AWS), the on-demand cloud-computing services firm. The intention is to roll out the pilot nationally across major cities in the UK.

Korean Government Network

The Korean government wanted to integrate each of its department's separate networks into a single network for operational efficiency and enhanced security. SK Broadband (a Seoul-based telecommunications company and a wholly owned subsidiary of SK Telecom) and its partner, IDQ (a Swiss quantum communications firm), developed a QKD network between government departments across 800 km, making it the largest quantum cryptography network outside China as of 2024 (ID Quantique Newsroom, 2022). A quantum key management system has been installed to monitor and control dozens of QKD nodes in real time, and to respond to the changing requirements of telecom operators. The plan is to extend the network to other government agencies and the private sector.

Airbus and European Quantum Communication Infrastructure (EuroQCI) Initiative

The European Quantum Communication Infrastructure (EuroQCI, 2024) is an initiative created to build a secure quantum communication infrastructure across the whole of the EU, including its overseas territories. EuroQCI comprises a terrestrial segment, using fibre communications networks linking strategic sites at national and cross-border levels, and a space segment, based on satellites. It will integrate quantum-based systems into existing communication infrastructure, providing an additional security layer to safeguard sensitive data and critical infrastructure. The goal is for EuroQCI to become the basis of a "quantum internet" in Europe, connecting quantum computers, simulators, and sensors via quantum networks. EuroQCI has selected a consortium of companies to study the design of the future European quantum communication network. The consortium, led by Airbus, consists of Leonardo, Orange, PwC France and Maghreb, Telespazio, the Consiglio Nazionale delle Ricerche (CNR), and the Istituto Nazionale di Ricerca Metrologica (INRiM). Quantum communication is an important domain for Airbus, given its synergies with classical optical communication systems, in which Airbus has experience (Airbus, 2023).

Quantum Network at Port of Rotterdam

The Port of Rotterdam has become a testbed for a quantum network that will enable secure internet connections between many users and stakeholders throughout the port area (portofrotterdam.com, 2022). For the busiest port in the region, malicious tapping of the communication systems between ships and operators can lead to significant financial losses, disruption of critical business operation, or physical harm. Hence, a quantum communication infrastructure will improve the safety of tens of thousands of sea ships and the security of the logistics chain. The quantum network technology is provided by Q*Bird, a spin-off of QuTech (an institute researching quantum computing between TNO and TU Delft).

Chicago's Quantum Network

A 124-mile quantum network connecting the University of Chicago and suburban labs has been built to provide a testbed for quantum security technology in the USA. The network distributes quantum keys over fibre-optic cable, using Toshiba's quantum security technology (University of Chicago.edu, 2022). The testbed offers a real-world environment to test new communication devices, security protocols, and quantum information transmission. For example, Toshiba is using the network to test its distributed quantum encryption keys, to understand the robustness of this method under environmental factors such as noise, weather, and temperature fluctuations (Chicagoquantum.org, 2022).

Singapore's National Quantum-Safe Network (NQSN)

The Singaporean government has launched a National Quantum-Safe Network (NQSN)—a nationwide platform of quantum-safe communication technologies (NUS.edu, 2022). The initiative provides infrastructure and a testbed for quantum network security for critical infrastructure, with applications for companies handling sensitive data in areas such as healthcare and finance. The project involves more than 15 public and private collaborators, including the National University of Singapore, Nanyang Technological University, Fraunhofer Singapore, AWS, and Singtel (nqsn.sg, 2024). The initial plan is to deploy 10 network nodes across Singapore, which will provide a public network that can act as a living lab for organisations wanting to explore quantum-safe communication technologies (Fraunhofer, 2022). The network will first investigate deployment of the quantum key distribution (QKD) technologies and post-quantum cryptography (PQC).

Quantum Key Distribution Satellite (QKDSat)

The aim of QKDSat, a project under the European Space Agency (ESA), is to implement quantum cryptography for secure satellite communication (eoPortal.com, 2021). Extending the reach of QKD beyond the Earth's atmosphere is a way to solve the limited travel range of a photon without compromising its integrity. Moreover, QKD in space through satellites could enable better data security for many industries that rely on satellite networks to transmit sensitive data, including the government and the military (Space.com, 2021). The technology has been developed by Arqit, a British cyber-security software developer.

Thales

French multinational company Thales carried out a pilot in 2023, successfully experimenting with end-to-end encrypted phone calls, tested to be resilient in the post-quantum era (Thales, 2023). Citing concerns of "store now, decrypt later" and potential vulnerabilities in public key cryptography, Thales created a proof of concept combining its Cryptosmart application and a 5G SIM employing hybrid cryptography. CRYSTALS-Kyber, one of the four algorithms selected by NIST, is the PQC algorithm natively implemented in the 5G SIM and used by the Cryptosmart application to encrypt the communication.

Apple

In 2024, Apple introduced what it described as "the most significant cryptographic security upgrade in iMessage history with the introduction of PQ3" (Apple, 2024). iMessage is Apple's native messaging application, and PQ3 is its latest messaging protocol. Using a hybrid design that combines new post-quantum algorithms with current elliptic curve algorithms, PQ3 uses PQC to secure both the initial key establishment and the ongoing message exchange, with the ability to rapidly and automatically restore the cryptographic security of a conversation, even if a given key is compromised.

Business, Economic, and Management Implications

Despite the technical challenges, quantum communication has demonstrated promising business value and commercial market potential (Cusumano, 2022).[1] This has significant implications for economics, business, and management.

One of the major societal issues with quantum communications is whether the technology should act as a "public good" that enables other benefits to be developed, or as a "private good". For example, the case for public infrastructure can be understood from the development of the Digital Public Infrastructure (DPI) in India, based on the digital stack (Panagariya, 2022). In 2010, the Indian government developed

[1] A recent report by McKinsey projects substantial revenue of close to USD8 billion by 2023 (Batra et al., 2021).

a digital national identity card, Aadhaar, which was issued to over 1.2 billion people in India, enabling identification by iris or thumb-print recognition via a simple Wi-Fi-enabled device connected to a central database. The Aadhaar system offered various benefits to the citizens of India, including voter identification and the ability for the government to transfer subsidies to the population directly. Moreover, the DPI enabled new payment systems to be built, such as the Unified Payments Interface (UPI), which allows inter-bank peer-to-peer and peer-to-merchant transactions. Such developments in the payment infrastructure allowed India to build new e-commerce businesses and tools that would scale across the whole nation, such as the Open Network for Digital Commerce (ONDC), which enables suppliers and buyers to connect to the network through open, interoperable systems. It provides unbundled products and services to customers traditionally left out of the e-commerce proposition (e.g., small/medium-sized enterprises). Hence, the DPI enabled other innovations to take place on the Indian digital stack.

Keeping this example in mind, we ask: Is quantum communication a private architecture that should be developed by private firms or a public architecture that needs to be subsidised by government to develop the equivalent of a DPI? If the latter, would it enable other innovations to take place, with various societal benefits?

The USA and the UK/Europe have adopted different stances on building a quantum communications infrastructure. The UK and Europe view QKD as a stepping stone for a more practical quantum network to connect quantum computers in the future. The USA, on the other hand, believes the interim step to building a QKD network is not necessary, particularly as it has limitations when it comes to verifying the authenticity of parties in the communication. Hence, the USA moved directly to building a quantum-ready network (i.e. a network that utilises PQC). The benefits of building a QKD network first, or going directly to the quantum-ready network, require further consideration.

It is foreseeable that quantum and classical protocols will co-exist and function in parallel to enable secure communication in the near term, while the benefits of such hybrid structures have not been fully explored (Gyongyosi & Imre, 2022; Kong et al., 2024). This creates opportunities to consider the dynamic interactions between classical legacy ecosystems and the quantum ecosystem, such as how their interoperability will be enacted through institutional, economic, political, and managerial efforts to facilitate efficient communication or manage cyber-security threats.

Telecoms and "data at rest" (network storage, etc.) providers are likely to be key in these questions. Most classical data users no longer expect to develop their own encryption and security protocols, relying instead on security provided at the storage and network levels. We should expect this to hold true with quantum communications; hence, the role of telecoms, network, and storage infrastructure players is crucial.

Leveraging quantum communication technologies to transition to a quantum-safe reality is challenging. Studies have implied that critical challenges need to be addressed across different levels in the multi-level perspective. For example, there is a lack of clarity around the role of funding players and strategies in driving the commercialisation of QKD. There is also a lack of political guidance (Travagnin & Lewis, 2018), as well as unclear governance and management support (Barker et al., 2021; Buchholz et al., 2020; Vermaas, 2017) and unreliable technology performance (Peet & O'Connor et al., 2018; Vermeer, 2020). In an organisational context, quantum communication can improve performance. For instance, in the case of high-frequency trading, team members' decision-making could be coordinated using entangled quantum signals across distances, which could result in improved performance compared to classical communication channels in the context of fast-changing prices (Brandenburger & La Mura, 2016). This indicates the potential application of quantum communication in advancing organisational decision support systems, which creates significant opportunities to improve performance. However, adopting quantum communication in organisations also encompasses various challenges and barriers. Kong et al. (2024) have identified some of these organisational challenges, categorised into four critical hurdles that impede quantum safety, including:

- the complexity of public key infrastructure interdependencies and standardisation
- a lack of awareness and urgency around quantum safety
- a shortage of reliable hardware and software
- unclear direction on governance and regulation.

For example, the complexity of public key infrastructure is shaped by multiple interdependent parties such as software providers, standards entities (e.g., the Internet Engineering Task Force (IETF)) and the World Wide Web Consortium (W3C)), governments, service and product providers, and end users. This has led to a low degree of interoperability between old and new encryption levels, and created challenges for the implementation of quantum-safe solutions. The lack of clarity around quantum-safe governance and regulation also creates issues, since organisations have no clear direction and tend to hold back from being the first mover.

Besides these challenges, the organisational adoption of quantum communication has many uncertainties and trade-offs. Successful quantum communication adoption requires technological maturity, and the high cost also poses a barrier for potential buyers (Cavaliere et al., 2020). Organisations with requirements for safe communication have been actively exploring new use cases and potential adoption of quantum-safe solutions, even before the technology fully matures (Batra et al., 2021). This illustrates the need to investigate the dynamics of quantum communications adoption when there are uncertainties about the maturity of the underlying technology, and the need to consider how it could be successfully adopted in industry while the technology is being developed.

It is essential to understand how to successfully commercialise quantum communication technologies and how they could generate economic value for firms or organisations. Some of the most serious challenges remain around scattered and small markets, supply chain development issues, technology validation and certification, a lack of available or adequate infrastructure, and after-sales services (Al Natsheh et al., 2015). For example, the value capture of the initial market for quantum communications is difficult to assess, as high-technology products can take a long time to grow their market size. In addition, the utility of performance of quantum communications also requires clearer benchmarks and evaluations. Lee et al. (2024) have proposed an initial utility matrix model to evaluate the performance of quantum networks. Each quantum task is associated with a utility function, so that the aggregate utility can be used to measure the overall performance of a quantum network. The study shows that quantum devices could be made to scale up effectively and viably. Nevertheless, what remains unclear is the economic measurement of the quantum network utility, resource allocation, commercial viability, and many other performance-related characteristics of a quantum-safe network. For example, it is essential to understand how quantum network utility could contribute to shared computing networks and related resource allocation, such that the distributed demand can be effectively and efficiently addressed. These challenges warrant future research to investigate the profitability, performance, and sustainability of quantum communication technologies.

Furthermore, as cloud services become available for quantum computing, quantum communication can possibly provide users with advanced security as they compute within a distributed architecture, enabling possibilities of confidential information sharing using the 6G network (Rozenman et al., 2023; Singh et al., 2020). Given these advantages, it is essential to ensure a seamless and stable transition from classical to quantum communication to harness the benefits of quantum computing. Moreover, Gyongosi and Imre (2022) suggest that standardisation of the "quantum internet" and the associated roadmap need to be sufficiently developed and understood in order to define a uniform quantum communications strategy, while considering the dynamics of the changing requirements.

Developing quantum communications also suggests a "global race", with characteristics of both competition and collaboration. Although quantum communication is at an early stage of growth in its technology life cycle, several countries have made large investments, played distinctive roles in the global quantum communications value chain, and made significant progress. For example, China, the USA, Japan, and the UK are among the top patent assignees in quantum communications, and they have emphasised four emerging topics: photonics, transmission and measurement, QKD-related apps, and quantum random number generators (Liu et al., 2022). This indicates diverse technological competencies at the global level, which opens up research opportunities for cross-country collaboration and cooperation in the quantum communication field.

Quantum communication also offers new insights into socio-technical transformation research. As discussed in this chapter, quantum computers could bring a new level of threat to existing classical information infrastructure, and quantum communications could play a key role in mitigating such threats. It would therefore be worth investigating the interplay between how developing quantum computers spurs the growth of quantum communications, and vice versa. Moreover, the overlay of institutional and business models could incentivise or delay these developments, adding a broad issue of socio-technical aspects to the evolution of quantum communications.

Summary of Business Implications and Potential Research Questions

In this chapter, we considered the business opportunities for firms and organisations in relation to quantum communication technologies (e.g., QKD and the "quantum internet") and business research conducted in this area. Quantum communication provides a new and advanced level of communication security and confidentiality, but critical issues worthy of investigation remain at multiple levels.

At the macro level, we have shown that an increasing number of public and national-level initiatives are being established to foster the innovation practices of QKD and the quantum internet in industry. It would be interesting to explore how these initiatives and national programmes enable the realisation and development of quantum communication technologies, their innovation trajectories, and the role of governments or policy-makers in accelerating these practices. Quantum communication technologies rely on digital infrastructure to achieve their advantage: How could national-level initiatives help the integration of quantum and digital legacy systems? How will firms and organisations be incentivised by these macro-level forces? And how might this stimulate the framing of new national policies, programmes, and initiatives?

At the meso level, it is important for incumbent firms and organisations to understand the potential impact of quantum communication technologies on security-related business practices. We know that quantum computers could bring a new level of threat to the existing classical information infrastructure, and quantum communications could play a key role in mitigating such threats. It would therefore be interesting to explore how quantum communication technologies could improve incumbent firms' communication confidentiality, and how developing quantum computers could spur the growth of quantum communications, and vice versa. We also noted that firms may struggle to identify suppliers or consumers to build their quantum communication supply chain, largely because of the novelty of the technology to these stakeholders, and unclear modifications to their existing structure. What will be the supply chain dynamics of quantum communications?

Business models are crucial in enabling such meso-level changes and are thus deserving of scrutiny. Specifically, incumbent firms need to understand potential quantum communication applications and how they can strategically work with them. It is thus important for business and management research to consider what characterises the unique value of quantum communication technologies in different settings (e.g., logistics or security). How should such value be created and governed as quantum devices are connected over time? How should incumbent firms get networked at local, national, and international levels to effectively innovate their business model in the quantum communication domain?

At the micro level, quantum start-ups play a central role in advancing the technological innovation niches of quantum communication technologies. Owing to the interdependent nature of quantum and digital communications, future research could explore how quantum start-ups should work strategically on such hybrids. As quantum communication technologies are introduced by start-ups to incumbent firms, it would be interesting to consider how these firms should collaborate, and how this could challenge the conventional communications infrastructure and organisational architecture. We summarise these questions in Table 3.1.

In summary, quantum communications promise enhanced security in communications methods, which is essential to maintaining integrity and trust, while also allowing new application areas to develop that could transform society.

Table 3.1 Potential research questions around quantum communications

Level	*Sub-question*
Macro level	• How should public/national-level initiatives enable the realisation and development of QKD/the quantum internet and its integration with legacy systems towards a secure communication infrastructure? • How should these initiatives incentivise private firms and, in turn, reframe or stimulate new initiatives?
Meso level—in general	• How could QKD improve security for incumbent firms? • How should different components and layers be supplied and integrated into a quantum internet, enabling diverse quantum application synergies?
Meso level—in the specifics of business models	• What characterises the unique value of quantum communication technologies that transforms individuals, organisations, and society across many different settings (e.g., logistics or security)? • How should the value of quantum communications emerge and develop as quantum devices are connected over time?
Micro level	• How should quantum start-ups develop the hybrid quantum–classical design of QKD towards proof of concept with their partners? • How should start-ups introduce quantum communication technologies to incumbent firms? • How will the work of QKD start-ups challenge conventional communications infrastructure and organisational architecture design?

References

Airbus. (2023). Quantum technologies | Airbus. Retrieved April 26, 2024, from https://www.airbus.com/en/innovation/disruptive-concepts/quantum-technologies

Al Natsheh, A., Gbadegeshin, S. A., Rimpiläinen, A., Imamovic-Tokalic, I., & Zambrano, A. (2015). Identifying the challenges in commercializing high technology: A case study of quantum key distribution technology. *Technology Innovation Management Review, 5*(1).

Apple. (2024). https://security.apple.com/blog/imessage-pq3/

Barker, W., Polk, W., & Souppaya, M. (2021). Getting ready for post-quantum cryptography: Exploring challenges associated with adopting and using post-quantum cryptographic algorithms (No. NIST CSWP 15). US Department of Commerce.

Barz, S., kashefi, E., Broadbent, A., Fitzsimons, J. F., Zeilinger, A., & Walther, P. (2012). Demonstration of blind quantum computing. *Science, 335*(6606), 303–308.

Batra, G., Gschwendtner, M., Ostojic, I., Queirolo, A., Soller, H., & Wester, L. (2021). Shaping the long race in quantum communication and quantum sensing. McKinsey.com. https://www.mckinsey.com/industries/industrials-and-electronics/our-insights/shaping-the-long-race-in-quantum-communication-and-quantum-sensing

Bennett, C., & Brassard, G. (1984). Quantum cryptography: Public key distribution and coin tossing. *IEEE International Conference on Computers, Systems and Signal Processing, 175*, 8.

Bernstein, D. (2009). *Post-quantum cryptography*. Springer.

Brandenburger, A., & Mura, P. L. (2016). Team decision problems with classical and quantum signals. *Philosophical Transactions of the Royal Society A, 374*, 2058.

Buchholz, S., Mariani, J., Routh, A., Keyal, A., & Kishnani, P. (2020). *The realist's guide to quantum technology and national security*. Deloitte Insights.

Cavaliere, F., Prati, E., Poti, L., Muhammad, I., & Catuogno, T. (2020). Secure quantum communication technologies and systems: From labs to markets. *Quantum Reports, 2*(1), 80–106.

Chen, Y. A., Zhang, Q., Chen, T. Y., Cai, W. Q., Liao, S. K., Zhang, J., Chen, K., Yin, J., Ren, J. G., Chen, Z., & Han, S. L. (2021). An integrated space-to-ground quantum communication network over 4,600 kilometres. *Nature, 589*, 214–219.

Chicagoquantum.org. (2022). About | Chicago Quantum Exchange. Retrieved April 26, 2024, from https://chicagoquantum.org/about

Cusumano, M. A. (2022). From quantum computing to quantum communications. *Communications of the ACM, 66*(1), 24–27.

Drmota, P., Nadlinger, D. P., Main, D., Nichol, B. C., Ainley, E. M., Leichtle, D., Mantri, A., Kashefi, E., Srinivas, R., Araneda, G., & Ballance, C. J. (2024). Verifiable blind quantum computing with trapped ions and single photons. *Physical Review Letters, 132*, Article 150604.

Ekert, A. (1991). Quantum cryptography based on Bell's Theorem. *Physical Review Letters, 67*(6), 661–663.

eoPortal.com. (2021). *QKDSat (Quantum Key Distribution Satellite) – eoPortal*. Retrieved May 8, 2024, from https://www.eoportal.org/satellite-missions/qkdsat#qkdsat-quantum-key-distribution-satellite

ETSI. (2020). *Migration strategies and recommendations to Quantum Safe schemes*. https://www.etsi.org/deliver/etsi_tr/103600_103699/103619/01.01.01_60/tr_103619v010101p.pdf

EuroQCI. (2024). https://digital-strategy.ec.europa.eu/en/policies/european-quantum-communication-infrastructure-euroqci

EY. (2022). https://www.ey.com/en_uk/news/2022/04/bt-and-toshiba-launch-first-commercial-trial-of-quantum-secured-communication-services

Fraunhofer. (2022). *National Quantum-Safe Network (NQSN)*. Retrieved April 26, 2024, from https://www.fraunhofer.sg/en/about/solutions/national-quantum-safe-network--nqsn-.html

Gyongyosi, L., & Imre, S. (2022). Advances in the quantum internet. *Communications of the ACM, 65*(8), 52–63.

Haitjema, M. (2007). *A Survey of the Prominent Quantum Key Distribution Protocols*. https://www.semanticscholar.org/paper/A-Survey-of-the-Prominent-Quantum-Key-Distribution-Haitjema/d710d2027e0edfbf7a7da30fa22690867493ea85#citing-papers

HSBC (2023). *HSBC becomes first bank to join the UK's pioneering commercial quantum secure metro network*. https://www.hsbc.com/news-and-views/news/media-releases/2023/hsbc-becomes-first-bank-to-join-the-uks-pioneering-commercial-quantum-secure-metro-network

ID Quantique Newsroom. (2022). *IDQ and SK Broadband complete phase one of nation-wide Korean QKD Network*. https://www.idquantique.com/idq-and-sk-broadband-complete-phase-one-of-nation-wide-korean-qkd-network/

Kong, I., Janssen, M., & Bharosa, N. (2024). Realizing quantum-safe information sharing: Implementation and adoption challenges and policy recommendations for quantum-safe transitions. *Government Information Quarterly, 41*(1), Article 101884.

Lee, Y., Dai, W., Towsley, D., & Englund, D. (2024). Quantum network utility: A framework for benchmarking quantum networks. *PNAS*, *121*(17).

Liu, X., Huang, Y., Yan, Y., Chen, S., & Tai, X. (2022). The technological emergence of quantum communication: A bibliometric analysis. *Technology Analysis & Strategic Management,* 1–7.

Mosca, M., & Paini, M. (2023). *Quantum Threat Timeline Report*. https://globalriskinstitute.org/publication/2023-quantum-threat-timeline-report/

NCSC. (2020). *Next steps in preparing for post-quantum cryptography*. https://www.ncsc.gov.uk/whitepaper/next-steps-preparing-for-post-quantum-cryptography

NIST. (2016). *Report on Post-Quantum Cryptography*. https://nvlpubs.nist.gov/nistpubs/ir/2016/NIST.IR.8105.pdf

NIST. (2024). Announcing Issuance of Federal Information Processing Standards (FIPS) FIPS 203, Module-Lattice-Based Key-Encapsulation Mechanism Standard, FIPS 204, Module-Lattice- Based Digital Signature Standard, and FIPS 205, Stateless Hash-Based Digital Signature Standard. *Federal Register, 89*(157), 66052.

Nqsn.sg. (2024). *National Quantum-Safe Network – National Quantum-Safe Network*. Retrieved April 26, 2024, from https://www.nqsn.sg/

NSM-10. (2022). *National Security Memorandum on Promoting United States Leadership in Quantum Computing While Mitigating Risks to Vulnerable Cryptographic Systems*. https://www.whitehouse.gov/briefing-room/statements-releases/2022/05/04/national-security-memorandum-on-promoting-united-states-leadership-in-quantum-computing-while-mitigating-risks-to-vulnerable-cryptographic-systems/

NUS.edu. (2022). *Singapore to build National Quantum-Safe Network that provides robust cybersecurity for critical infrastructure*. Retrieved April 26, 2024, from https://news.nus.edu.sg/national-quantum-safe-network-that-provides-robust-cybersecurity/

O'Connor, L., Dukatz, C., DiValentin, L., & Farhady, N. (2018). Cryptography in a post-quantum world: preparing intelligent enterprises now for a secure future. Accenture Labs.

Panagariya, A. (2022). Digital revolution, financial infrastructure and entrepreneurship: The case of India. *Asia and the Global Economy, 2*(2), Article 100027.

Peet, E. D., & Vermeer, M. J. (2020). Securing communications in the quantum computing age: Managing the risks to encryption.

portofrotterdam.com. (2022). Untappable internet for Port of Rotterdam offered by quantum technology | Port of Rotterdam. Retrieved April 26, 2024, from https://www.portofrotterdam.com/en/news-and-press-releases/untappable-internet-for-port-of-rotterdam-offered-by-quantum-technology

Rozenman, G. G., Kundu, N. K., Liu, R., Zhang, L., Maslennikov, A., Reches, Y., & Youm, H. Y. (2023). The quantum internet: A synergy of quantum information technologies and 6G networks. *IET Quantum Communication, 4*(4), 147–166.

Sasaki, M., Fujiwara, M., Ishizuka, H., Klaus, W., Wakui, K., Takeoka, M., Miki, S., Yamashita, T., Wang, Z., Tanaka, A., & Yoshino, K. (2011). Field test of quantum key distribution in the Tokyo QKD Network. *Optics Express, 19*(11), 10387–10409.

Shor, P. W. (1994). Algorithms for quantum computation: Discrete logarithms and factoring. *Proceedings 35th Annual Symposium on Foundations of Computer Science* (pp. 124–134). IEEE Computer Society Press.

Singh, S. K., Azzaoui, A. E., Salim, M. M., & Park, J. H. (2020). Quantum communication technology for future ICT-review. *Journal of Information Processing Systems, 16*(6), 1459–1478.

Space.com. (2021). U.K. company to start sending secret quantum keys with satellites in 2023 | Space. Retrieved May 8, 2024, from https://www.space.com/arqit-quantum-key-distribution-space

Stucki, D., Legre, M., Buntschu, F., Clausen, B., Felber, N., Gisin, N., Henzen, L., Junod, P., Litzistorf, G., Monbaron, P., & Monat, L. (2011). Long-term performance of the SwissQuantum quantum key distribution network in a field environment. *New Journal of Physics, 13*, Article 123001.

Thales. (2023). *Thales pioneers Post Quantum Cryptography with a successful world-first pilot on phone calls.* https://www.thalesgroup.com/en/worldwide/digital-identity-and-security/press_release/thales-pioneers-post-quantum-cryptography

Travagnin, M., & Lewis, A. (2018). *The impact of quantum technologies on EU's future policies PART 2 Quantum Communications: from science to policies.*

University of Chicago.edu. (2022). *Chicago expands and activates quantum network, taking steps toward a secure quantum internet.* https://news.uchicago.edu/story/chicago-quantum-network-argonne-pritzker-molecular-engineering-toshiba

Velu, C., & Putra, F. H. (2023). How to introduce quantum computers without slowing economic growth. *Nature, 619*(7970), 461–464.

Vermaas, P. E. (2017). The societal impact of the emerging quantum technologies: A renewed urgency to make quantum theory understandable. *Ethics and Information Technology, 19*, 241–246.

Wehner, S., Elkouss, D., & Henson, R. (2018). Quantum Internet: A vision for the road ahead. *Science, 362*, eaam9288.

CHAPTER 4

Sensing, Imaging, and Timing: Sense, See, and Navigate a Complex World

This chapter covers:

- *An overview of sensing, imaging and timing;*
- *Why do quantum technologies have a role in:*
    - o *sensing and imaging?*
    - o *position, navigation, and timing (PNT) (including protecting critical national infrastructure)?*
- *An outline of some initial deployment/exploration of quantum for sensing and imaging and PNT applications;*
- *A discussion of the possible business and economic implications using the frameworks outlined in Chapter 1;*
- *An outline of research questions to be explored further.*

Introduction

Quantum sensing, imaging, and timing is a broad range of tools—in some ways, it is the most established field in quantum technologies. It includes areas such as:

- gravimetry—measurements of tiny variations in gravity with applications in mineral exploration and navigation

C. Velu et al., *The Business of Quantum Technologies*,
https://doi.org/10.1007/978-3-031-99808-9_4

- inertial navigation—navigation that does not rely on GPS or similar systems
- quantum magnetometry—ultra-sensitive sensors for detecting magnetic fields, with applications in medical imaging, position-finding, and geology
- high-resolution microscopy—imaging of, for example, biological systems
- quantum lidar—with applications in, for example, detecting gas leaks, non-line-of-sight imaging
- atomic clocks—used in navigation and time synchronisation.

These, in turn, have applications in climate change, healthcare, defence, space, and transportation. We begin by considering classical sensing technology and then provide an overview of the major areas of quantum sensing, imaging, and timing.

What Is a Quantum Sensor?

Let us first consider sensing technologies. Classical digital sensors are designed to respond to an input parameter such as temperature, air pressure, or acceleration, to digitise that information, and to produce an output, such as a voltage or a digital representation. They rely on physical processes in the bulk material of the sensor that are affected by the variable of interest, meaning very large number of atoms are involved. Quantum sensors typically rely on just one or a few (compared to bulk materials) quantum states being affected by the external variable, and those quantum states may be either a few atoms or sometimes photons (i.e., light). They often use quantum superposition, and some use quantum entanglement. Quantum sensors are generally used to measure the same phenomena as classical sensors, but their quantum nature allows them, in principle, to have much higher sensitivity or precision and stability.

Like qubits, quantum sensors require discrete quantum states, realised by polarisation of photons, quantised currents in superconducting circuits or electronic or nuclear spin states, for example. Also, like qubits, these states must be initialised to a known state, using optical, microwave or radio frequency signals, and a quantum sensor must provide a way of reading out the quantum state. Unlike qubits, quantum sensing requires the quantum states to interact strongly with their environment.

Quantum Gravimetry

Gravimeters are sensors that measure the strength of a gravitational field. A simple spring balance or set of weighing scales is a gravimeter, which works by measuring the extension of a spring when a mass is applied. More accurate classical gravimeters typically work by measuring the acceleration of a test mass when dropped in a vacuum. Quantum gravimeters typically work more like this second type of classical gravimeter, but instead of using a test mass, they use ultra-cold atoms dropped in the gravitational field. However, they also typically split the falling atoms into packets that fall independently, but then recombine them and measure the resulting quantum interference effects, which occur according to the principles of quantum superposition discussed in Chapter 1.

Using ultra-cold atoms as test masses has the advantage that all atoms of a given element are guaranteed to be identical and unchanging. Unlike manufactured test masses, which can wear out, individual atoms maintain their properties (including their mass) indefinitely, requiring no maintenance. Furthermore, the interferometry process used when packets of atoms recombine can be used to quickly identify and remove vibrations, which might otherwise mask interesting gravitational features. Stray et al. used this technique to survey an underground tunnel with a reported statistical uncertainty of $2 \times 10^{-8}/s^2$. They demonstrated effective suppression of vibrations, hence reducing the time required to take such measurements compared to classical techniques, and showed the potential of the technique for underground mapping (Stray et al., 2022). The Quantum Technology Potential for Railway Infrastructure project (QT-PRI, 2023) estimates that there are over 190,000 earthworks and buried infrastructure associated with UK railways alone, which severely impacts surveying times when maintaining rail infrastructure built on top; this reduction in measurement time suggests the potential of quantum gravimetry in civil engineering. Similarly, this technology could be used in energy and mineral or aquifer exploration, particularly where classical gravimetry techniques are not sensitive enough to detect small deposits. The same technology was later tested in sea trials, which provides initial evidence that such systems could be used in inertial navigation systems that do not rely on GPS.

Quantum Inertial Sensing

Classical inertial sensors have many applications in determining orientation, rotation, and acceleration, for example, in mobile phones, smart watches, and automotive. They may be used for navigation when combined with a way of getting a "fix" (e.g., by connecting to a GPS satellite), but typically they have large levels of drift, so if a fix is not regularly updated, it rapidly loses accuracy.

Quantum inertial sensors, based on techniques similar to those used in quantum gravimetry, potentially have far greater accuracy than classical techniques, greatly reducing the need to take a fix at regular intervals (e.g., Wright et al., 2022). This reduces the dependence on GPS, which requires a clear line of sight to the satellite and hence cannot be used in some indoor environments or underground. GPS can also be jammed relatively easily, or it could be withdrawn as a service (see discussion later in this chapter).

However, despite their advantages, quantum inertial sensors currently refresh rather slowly, at the order of a few times per second, compared with classical inertial technology, which can often refresh at close to 1,000 times per second. During this "dead time" of the order of 0.1–0.5 seconds, a quantum inertial sensor can provide no useful information, and research is ongoing to determine whether quantum and classical inertial sensors could be combined to overcome this limitation. Templier et al. (2022) report a 50-fold improvement in bias stability using these hybrid quantum–classical techniques, opening the door to underground inertial navigation and improvements to air and maritime navigation.

Quantum Magnetometry

Magnetometry is the measurement of magnetic fields. Very small changes in the magnitude or direction of a magnetic field can induce quantum effects, meaning magnetometers based on quantum effects can be extremely sensitive. Quantum magnetic sensors were first developed in the 1960s. Josephson (1962) developed a theoretical explanation of how electrical currents can flow with zero resistance across superconducting materials separated by a thin, insulating barrier. Soon afterwards, Anderson and Rowell implemented the so-called Josephson junction in hardware (Anderson & Rowell, 1964), confirming Josephson's predictions, and within months, Jaklevic and collaborators had used the

Josephson junction to develop the superconducting quantum interference device (SQUID) (Jaklevic et al., 1964).

Electrical signals in the brain generate minute magnetic fields, which SQUIDs can detect, meaning they have been a crucial tool in brain-scanning techniques. However, they tend to be bulky devices, with complex super-cooling requirements. More recently, optically pumped magnetometers (OPMs) have been developed, which use laser light to "pump" atoms into specific quantum states. These do not typically require super-cooling, so they tend to be much smaller devices, with lower maintenance costs and simpler deployment.

Quantum Imaging (Microscopy and Lidar)

Classical imaging typically illuminates an object and then collects and measures that same light. Quantum entanglement, in principle, allows new forms of imaging, where an object can be illuminated with a set of photons that have been quantum entangled with other photons, and those other photons are collected and measured, sometimes referred to as "ghost imaging" (Padgett & Boyd, 2017). Why should this be useful? It turns out that many compounds are more easily detectable in the infrared range, but many detectors operate most efficiently in the visible spectrum. Using infrared photons entangled with visible light photons thereby offers cheaper visible light detectors, while the imaging is done in the infrared.

Quantum entanglement of photons has also found applications in light detection and ranging (lidar). Lidar apparatus emits laser pulses to a target and measures the reflected pulses. The time taken for the pulse to return to the detector can be used to estimate the range to the target, and the frequency of the reflected pulse can be used to calculate the relative velocity of the target to that of the detector, using the Doppler shift principle.[1] Quantum lidar techniques based on entanglement may be able to produce better precision and resolution than classical techniques (see, for example, Huang et al., 2023).

[1] The Doppler shift is readily observed in acoustics: a fast-moving object emitting a sound has an apparent higher pitch than a slowly moving object. This can be seen when a car drives past, and the apparent pitch of the sound drops at the point that the car passes the observer.

Quantum Clocks, Timing, and Positioning

Atomic clocks based on the resonant frequencies of certain atoms as they transition between quantum energy states have been used for many years. They are so accurate that in 1967 the second was redefined in terms of the transition frequency of an electron in a caesium 133 atom. Such clocks can be accurate to one second in tens of millions of years (compare this with a quartz wristwatch, which can drift by tens of seconds over the course of a few weeks).

Other atoms with higher resonant frequencies are being investigated. Scandium has a transition frequency of the order of 1,000 times that of caesium, meaning a scandium-based clock could have an accuracy of around one second in a hundred billion years, substantially longer than the age of the universe.

Atomic clocks are used in several infrastructure-level applications. For example, they are used to generate the timing for high-speed internet. As network speeds increase with the roll-out of 5G and 6G telecommunications, accurate timing becomes even more important. They have further applications in timing for the Global Positioning System (GPS). Society's reliance on satellite-based GPS or global navigation satellite systems (GNSS) for timing and location information has become ubiquitous (Milner, 2017).

Most people do not appreciate their everyday reliance on GPS or GNSS via their mobile phones or when they call an Uber to take them home. The GPS system was initially developed by the USA during the Cold War, following the launch of the Sputnik satellite in 1957 by the Soviet Union (Milner, 2017; RTS International, 2019). The resulting space race led the USA to accelerate the scientific development of equipment for US national security. Researchers discovered they could identify the location of ground-receiving stations based on Sputnik's radio transmission, and hence determine the satellite's orbit. This led to the development of satellite-based systems at US national labs and among private-sector firms. The initial use was thought to be for the purpose of more accurate navigation of maritime vessels. However, willingness to invest in developing the GPS system was limited because of the low need for accurate positioning and navigation from both the US Navy and US Air Force, respectively (Milner, 2017). Neither the Navy nor the Air Force felt they needed a more accurate navigation system, as they knew the location of their aircrafts and ships reasonably precisely. Hence, there was a reluctance to support the budget for developing GPS. A further hurdle was the US Air Force corporate culture: pilots who were part of the senior team were sceptical about spending for GPS development, as there would be less funding for piloted aircraft.

However, support for GPS changed when it was reframed from being a navigation system to a guidance system (Milner, 2017). The main impetus came from ethical considerations for the US Armed Forces to have accurate missile guiding so as not to carpet-bomb cities during the Iraq war. This prompted the development of satellites to transmit GPS signals. As GPS was being developed for military use, a concurrent need developed for its use in sugar-beet agriculture, a crucial crop in the USA (Milner, 2017). Sugar from the beet crop is a key ingredient for food additives, livestock feed, and biofuels. It was estimated that during the planting, nurturing, and harvesting seasons, accurately tracking the movement of farming equipment using GPS signals could significantly enhance crop yields and thus help with agricultural productivity. Hence, the US government decided to develop two codes for the use of GPS: the precision (P) code for military use with enhanced security encryption; and a coarse acquisition (C/A) code for civil use with less security.

In 1996, President Clinton delivered on the promise of President Reagan to make GPS available for civilian use at no cost. This followed Korean Airlines Flight 007 being shot down for flying too close to Soviet airspace. Since then, three other major satellite systems globally have been developed, operated by the European Union (Galileo), Russia (GLONASS), and China (BeiDou).

Developing the C/A code enabled free global distribution of positioning and timing information to the general public based on GPS satellites. The GPS system consists of around thirty satellites that synchronise their time with various control stations, which coordinate with a master clock and correct for time and positioning information. The US Naval Observatory is tasked with maintaining the time and frequency of the GPS system. To pinpoint location, GPS receivers such as our phones need to receive messages from a minimum of four satellites to calibrate the location and timing. Many industries rely on GPS for their service delivery, including electricity to enable the stability and efficiency of the transmission, finance for high-frequency trading, precision agriculture, maritime for navigation and port operations, telecommunications for improved bandwidth utilisation, and transportation for logistics.

Therefore, much critical national infrastructure (CNIs) relies on GPS signals.

However, GPS signals are liable to disruption by weather storms, jamming (where the receiver does not receive the GPS signals), and spoofing (where false signals are transmitted). The number of occurrences of weather-related events, and jamming and spoofing activities, has increased. For example, there has been increased jamming of GPS signals in the Baltic Sea, affecting thousands of planes flying in the region (Wired, 2024). Moreover, recent geomagnetic weather storms have affected the accuracy of tracking agricultural equipment used in the USA (John Deere News, 2024). However, the broad costs of disturbances to GPS signals that affect CNIs are often borne by society as a whole, while the benefits accrue to individual firms. This results in misaligned incentives between firms that rely on free GPS signals to provide services (effectively paid for by US taxpayers), and society more broadly (Lobo, Paul and Velu, 2025). The cost of the misaligned incentives is very high, as it affects the resilience of the CNI for stakeholders such as emergency services, financial services, and energy transmission, among others.

There is an increasing move to develop localised clocks and distribution of time locally to act as holdovers in the event of such disruptions. It is also possible that local clocks could become the primary system, and GPS could provide a holdover back-up system. For example, the National Physical Laboratory in the UK provides local timing to the financial markets in London, distributed using fibre-optic cables from their stations. The next generation of these "timing as a service" systems could provide even more accurate timing using quantum clocks that use optical wavelengths than atomic clocks that use microwaves. Such a system could be rolled out to the rest of the nation, potentially stimulating other innovative services based on more accurate timing services, such as autonomous vehicles or new types of financial service based on calibrating with the timing system of the stock exchange.

Business Case Studies

In this section, we review some of the emerging use cases related to quantum-based sensing, imaging, and timing applications.

Brain Imaging and UK QST HUB's OPM-MEG System

Brain imaging has become increasingly important for many issues in healthcare. The fundamental challenge is the complexity of the brain; given this complexity, it is hard to accurately detect brain impulses using conventional techniques. However, quantum sensing technologies can be used to precisely measure weak signals of neuronal activities. Using optically pumped magnetometers (OPMs), engineers and physicists from the UK Quantum Sensing and Timing Hub have created the first wearable magnetoencephalography (MEG) system that can be directly put on the scalp, allowing free movement during scanning (quantumsensors.org, 2018). This OPM-based MEG technology is outperforming many conventional MEG systems using SQUID techniques. It substantially reduces costs and overheads and is demonstrating transformative potential in detection and diagnosis in brain research, including dementia and Parkinson's. Cerca Magnetics, a spin-out of the University of Nottingham (part of the aforementioned hub) has partnered with the Hospital for Sick Children in Toronto, and its wearable OPM-MEG system is now being used to research autism in young children (Cerca Magnetics, 2021).

Satellite-Based Gravity Sensing and CASPA

Using satellites to measure gravity is increasingly important in understanding and predicting natural disasters such as earthquakes, volcanic activities, and flooding (Tralli et al., 2005). However, classical gravity measurement approaches usually provide low-resolution images because of the low spatial resolutions of classical sensors. To address such problems, an Innovate UK project, Cold Atom Space Payload (CASPA), explored the use of quantum gravimeters, in a partnership between the University of Birmingham, the University of Southampton's Optical Research Centre, Cohesion, XCAM, Clyde Space, and Gooch & Housego (Fryer, 2018).

Underwater Imaging and QuantIC

Underwater imaging includes mapping underwater terrain. This is challenging because of the low visibility in deep water (Bessell-Browne et al., 2017). Current underwater imaging techniques have limited resolution quality, especially when it comes to mapping moving targets under the sea. Using quantum sensing technologies, research teams from QuantIC delivered a fully submerged underwater lidar transceiver system using single-photon-detection techniques, achieving a 3D image of moving objects in turbid underwater environments (QuantIC, 2024). The team is in industrial-academic collaboration across diverse organisations and disciplines. The University of Edinburgh designed and provided the single-photon techniques, and Heriot-Watt University developed the overall system. Researchers with backgrounds in underwater robotics, laser sources, detector design, manufacturing, and software development have also been involved. The delivered system was able to capture images of underwater moving objects at distances of up to 7.5 attenuation lengths from the transceiver. This provides transformative potential in many application areas such as defence and security, offshore site surveys, and marine science.

Atomic Clocks and QuantX

QuantX Labs, a private Australian company working on timing and sensing products, has partnered with Surrey Satellite Technology Limited (SSTL), a global company in satellite technology, through Airbus Australia, to co-explore quantum timing solutions with optical atomic clocks (QuantX, 2023). SSTL provides space systems with engineering expertise and is also a conduit for the skill sets of the QuantX engineering team and the wider skills base of Australia's space sector (Lotfourteen, 2023). The collaboration has been supported by the Australian government through its Demonstrator Program. QuantX Labs is envisioned to demonstrate precision timing technology by 2026.

Quantum Detectors and Autonomous Vehicles

With classical optical sensors, lidar can accurately find the position of objects and determine the distances between them. However, current classical technologies usually have poor sensitivity to low levels of reflected light. The University of Glasgow has partnered with Heriot-Watt University and is developing a single-photon avalanche diode that could be produced at extremely low cost and would be an important component of a quantum lidar system (QuantIC, 2022). They have used affordable silicon and germanium platforms to develop an eye-safe laser system that can be used in demanding environments such as rain and dust.

Quantum Gas Camera Lidar

QLM Tec, a spin-off company from the University of Bristol, has developed a Quantum Gas Lidar, a novel technology for methane emissions quantification (CSA Catapult.org.uk, 2023). QLM's system offers a novel tool for industries reliant on accurate gas monitoring, such as oil and gas, agriculture, and environmental conservation (Millington-Smith, 2023). QLM's Quantum Gas Lidar enables proactive intervention and precise quantification, essential for informed decision-making and regulatory compliance, including detecting fugitive emissions in industrial facilities, and monitoring methane leaks in natural gas pipelines (QLMtec.com, 2024). Furthermore, the Quantum Gas Lidar has implications for environmental conservation, such as monitoring methane emissions from landfills or agricultural activities.

Quantum Gravity Sensors for Underground Sensing

Traditional methods of underground sensing, such as seismic surveys or ground-penetrating radar, have limitations in resolution and depth penetration. Quantum gravity sensors, however, exploit the quantum properties of atoms to measure minute variations in gravitational fields (Bongs et al., 2023). These sensors, often based on cold atom interferometry, can detect subtle differences in density below the Earth's surface, providing detailed and accurate maps of underground formations. These principles have been leveraged by a Birmingham University spin-off company, Delta-G, which has developed a quantum gravity gradiometry platform (delta-g.co.uk, 2023). There are several applications of quantum gravity sensors, from geological mapping and resource exploration to infrastructure monitoring and environmental assessment. For instance, they can identify hidden geological features that are crucial for oil, gas, and mineral exploration, monitor sub-surface conditions for construction projects, and help with archaeological investigations by revealing buried structures without excavation (Quantumsensors.org, 2022).

Business, Economic, and Management Implications

Given the unprecedented potential accuracy of measurement, quantum sensing technologies may offer important benefits to business, economics, and management. Quantum sensing technologies may enable asset maintenance and control by precisely detecting unusual events in the multitude of variables that track organisations' technological asset performance. Quantum sensors could detect signals of equipment failures with extreme sensitivity and reliability or provide opportunities to accurately assess and predict equipment performance, which would reduce costs and mitigate technology failure risks (Crawford et al., 2021). For instance, invasive vector magnetic imaging can provide high spatial resolution and wide field of view through NV-diamond quantum sensors, which could enable precise and accurate detection of faults in new material design (Gschwendtner et al., 2024). In addition, in the water sector, water quality and pressure can be more precisely and accurately monitored in water and sewage infrastructure with quantum magnetometers or atomic spectrometers, leading to more timely control and prediction of water power (Kantsepolsky & Aviv, 2024).

Quantum sensing technologies may improve legacy system sustainability, efficiency, and security. For example, electricity transmission and storage usually require close monitoring and timely responses; it may be possible to improve these with quantum sensing technologies by precisely monitoring electric grid performance. As a result, the consumption of energy or electricity flows could be better monitored using a series of quantum sensors, enabling more efficient and safer energy usage for organisations (Crawford et al., 2021).

In transportation systems, quantum sensing could provide precise, real-time traffic data using quantum accelerometers and quantum strain gauges. These could help to optimise dynamic routine planning and transportation operations, resulting in more sustainable urban mobility (Hassani & Dackermann, 2023; Kantsepolsky & Aviv, 2024).

The data from quantum sensors could enhance training for AI and machine-learning techniques (Gschwendtner et al., 2024). Furthermore, quantum metrology could accelerate the building of complex emerging technologies such as quantum computers, where error correction could be tested more effectively, improving energy efficiency during the construction of quantum computers (Martinis, 2015).

Quantum sensing technologies may be able to revolutionise communication systems with quantum timing applications (Bongs et al., 2023). Such precision could substantially reduce data transmission requirements and data latency (Kantsepolsky & Aviv, 2024).

Quantum sensing technologies are also enabling new forms of collaboration. For example, Gschwendtner et al. (2024) argue that quantum sensing technologies have shaped a unique ecosystem where researchers, start-ups, and industry leaders jointly engage in quantum sensing exploration. Many nations, including the UK, USA, and Germany, have also set up large-scale collaboration projects among government sectors, academia, and industry to support cross-boundary knowledge exchange to meet national goals around quantum sensing (Bongs et al., 2023; Gupta et al., 2022). For instance, the QuantumBW innovation initiative was created to facilitate quantum sensing adoption in Germany, with a focus on education and training, ecosystem design, location marketing, and quantum infrastructure.

Despite these potential upsides, quantum sensing technologies also face challenges that limit their commercialisation and adoption in society. First, it remains challenging to adopt quantum sensing technologies in real-world environments because of the complexity of the environmental system. This can impede a quantum sensor's robustness and performance (Crawford et al., 2021). In addition, it remains unclear how, when, and where quantum sensors can be introduced to the market with high reliability, manufacturing reproducibility, cost effectiveness, and compatibility with other systems in use (Bongs et al., 2023). It is therefore essential not only to advance the technical maturity of quantum sensing to enhance its performance but also to consider diverse socio-technical aspects in design before mass-producing quantum sensing materials. Currently, quantum sensing technologies have exhibited advantages in research laboratories, while such transformative value has not been captured in the business and management domains. Therefore, more business and management research is needed to investigate innovation processes and trajectories that could bring quantum sensing technologies from research into real-life settings.

Second, while quantum sensing can improve classical sensors' performance, they must be integrated with classical systems to unlock their full potential to empower the legacy system (Gschwendtner et al., 2024). However, the integration between quantum materials and classical devices remains challenging because of the multitude of environmental variables and inter-operational complexity. Therefore, it is important to understand quantum–classical integration dynamics across multiple levels as quantum sensing is introduced in society.

Third, owing to the nature of quantum sensing, collaborations that shape quantum innovation require the establishment of distinctive networks and ecosystems, new strategies, new knowledge skills, and coordination modes to enable its adoption in society. For example, the role of government is important, and quantum sensing technologies have received less attention from national quantum initiatives than other quantum technologies (Bongs et al., 2023). Policies and regulations that enable quantum sensing innovation are unclear, particularly in the management areas of national quantum sensing infrastructure. Educating talented people with quantum-sensing-relevant knowledge and skills is essential, as quantum-sensing market growth could outpace talent availability (Gschwendtner et al., 2024). Moreover, systems integrators are key to enabling the introduction of quantum sensing into society (Gschwendtner et al., 2024). This warrants future management research.

Lastly, it remains unclear how to capture the value of quantum sensing in both the short and long terms, which suggests the need for new business models and new management strategies. Given that quantum sensing might provide a lucrative market, developing a disruptive, forward-looking mindset with distinct business strategies is key to driving quantum sensing from research into real-life applications (Gschwendtner et al., 2024).

Summary of Business Implications and Potential Research Questions

Quantum sensing technologies such as timing and imaging have enabled advanced precision that could benefit society in many ways (e.g., GPS, transportation). However, although the technology provides profound opportunities for firms to deliver and capture value, the issues indicated above warrant future research to explore the business and management aspects of the technology through multi-level perspectives.

At the macro level, because of the relatively low priority and urgency of quantum sensing at national or public levels compared to other quantum application areas, it is important to ask why and how government and public policy-makers should design and promote clear national guidance to support the development of quantum sensing technologies.

Many sensing applications in the market are based on classical technologies. Therefore, how can government promote quantum sensing industry development that is cheaper and more effective than existing solutions? The high precision of quantum sensing could also enable accurate and timely control of environmental resources (e.g., energy). How could quantum sensing technologies influence the sustainability of society?

At the meso level, we have shown that firms are fostering multi-interdisciplinary partnerships to co-explore quantum sensing technologies, and to shape dynamic supply chains. It is therefore interesting to consider how these cross-disciplinary collaborations in the field of quantum sensing stimulate customer purchasing and industrial economic growth. How should resource assignments across diverse quantum sensing projects be strategically aligned to create value? Business models might provide a useful lens to answer these questions. It is thus important to ask how firms should design their business models to capture the transformative value of quantum sensing technologies in complex systems through interdisciplinary collaboration (e.g., engineers, physicists, business). When and how should quantum sensing technologies be spun out of research laboratories to start creating business value for industries?

At the micro level, quantum start-ups are key to driving the niche design of quantum sensing technologies corresponding to existing digital infrastructure. It would be interesting to explore how quantum start-ups play a role in integrating quantum sensing applications and digital devices. What interplay of dynamics is required at the niche level? A quantum approach to sensors might be an incremental improvement, while radical change may occur when different types of quantum sensing technology work together (e.g., metrology, timing, imaging) in an interconnected ecosystem. How will these niche innovations challenge the conventional socio-technical regime and create new windows of opportunity for radical change? We summarise these questions in Table 4.1.

Sensing, imaging, and timing technologies are often embedded in the daily lives of members of society without much notice, but they have profound implications when they do not function or can be improved.

Table 4.1 Potential research questions around quantum sensing, imaging, and timing

Level	*Sub-question*
Macro level	• How should government and public policy authors design and promote national policies to support the development of quantum sensing technologies to provide a step-change improvement to existing sensing, imaging, and timing technologies? • How could quantum sensing technologies influence the sustainability of society, across aspects such as energy consumption or agricultural work?
Meso level—in general	• How could multidisciplinary partnerships in the field of quantum sensing stimulate customer purchasing and industrial economic growth? • How should resource assignments across diverse quantum sensing projects be strategically aligned to create value?
Meso level—in the specifics of business models	• How is the transformative value of quantum sensing technologies in complex systems developed through interdisciplinary collaboration (e.g., engineers, physicists, business)? • When and how should quantum sensing technologies be spun out of research laboratories to start creating business value for industries?
Micro level	• How do quantum start-ups promote the hybrid design of quantum sensing applications corresponding to digital devices/infrastructure? • How should quantum start-ups collaborate with research institutions to enhance quantum timing technologies? • How could multiple innovation niches in different quantum sensing technologies (e.g., sensing, timing, imaging) synergise as a new opportunity to enable both incremental and radical improvement of the conventional socio-technical regime?

Quantum-based sensing, imaging, and timing could provide a step change in performance and resilience and have a transformative impact on society. However, the challenge is to provide the economic incentives and manage the risk to replace existing classical systems with quantum-based technologies. New industrial systems and business models need to be nurtured as the technology matures in order to overcome this challenge.

References

Anderson, P. W., & Rowell, J. M. (1964). Probable observation of the Josephson superconducting tunnelling effect. *Physical Review Letters, 10*, 23.

Bessell-Browne, P., Negri, A. P., Fisher, R., Clode, P. L., & Jones, R. (2017). Impacts of light limitation on corals and crustose coralline algae. *Scientific Reports, 7*(1), 11553.

Bongs, K., Bennett, S., & Lohmann, A. (2023). Quantum sensors will start a revolution—if we deploy them right. *Nature, 617*(7962), 672–675.

Cerca Magnetics. (2021). https://www.cercamagnetics.com/articles/sickkids-system-installation

Crawford, S. E., Shugayev, R. A., Paudel, H. P., Lu, P., Syamlal, M., Ohodnicki, P. R., & Duan, Y. (2021). Quantum sensing for energy applications: Review and perspective. *Advanced Quantum Technologies, 4*(8), 2100049.

CSA Catapult.org.uk. (2023). *CSA catapult—Case study: Enabling ground-breaking gas sensing technology to reduce the effects of climate change*. Retrieved May 14, 2024, from https://csa.catapult.org.uk/blog/2023/01/16/case-study-enabling-ground-breaking-gas-sensing-technology-to-reduce-the-effects-of-climate-change/

delta-g.co.uk. (2023). *Delta g—Leveraging gravity so we can see the unseen*. Retrieved May 28, 2024, from https://www.delta-g.co.uk/

Fryer, T. (2018). Cold atoms at space probe's heart [Space Sensor Technology]. *Engineering & Technology, 13*(1), 56–59.

Gschwendtner, M., Bormuth, Y., Soller, H., Stein, A., & Walsworth, R. L. (2024). Quantum sensing can already make a difference. But where? *Journal of Innovation Management, 12*(1).

Gupta, B. M., Dhawan, S. M., & Mamdapur, G. M. N. (2022). Quantum sensing research: A scientometric assessment of global publications during 1991–2020. *International Journal of Knowledge Content Development & Technology, 12*(3).

Hassani, S., & Dackermann, U. (2023). A systematic review of advanced sensor technologies for non-destructive testing and structural health monitoring. *Sensors, 23*(4), 2204.

Huang, M. et al. (2023). Quantum LiDAR with frequency modulated continuous wave, arXiv:2307.11590

Jaklevic, R. C., Lambe, J., Silver, A. H., & Mercereau, J. E. (1964). Quantum interference effects in Josephson tunnelling. *Physical Review Letters, 12*, 159.

John Deere News. (2024). *Geomagnetic storm affecting GPS signals, 11 May* https://landmarkimp.com/news/news/blog/geomagnetic-storm-affecting-gps-signals--may-2024/?ref=404media.co
Josephson, B. D. (1962). Possible new effects in superconductive tunnelling. *Physics Letters, 1*(7), 251–253.
Kantsepolsky, B., & Aviv, I. (2024). Sensors in civil engineering: From existing gaps to quantum opportunities. *Smart Cities, 7*(1), 277–301.
Lobo, L., Paul, D., Velu, C. (2025). GPS timekeeping in increasingly vulnerable: here's how to deliver future-proofed time. *Nature, 645*(8081), 585–588.
Lotfourteen. (2023). *QuantX labs and SSTL partner to propel Australian quantum clock technology into space*. https://lotfourteen.com.au/news/quantx-labs-and-sstl-partner-to-propel-australian-quantum-clock-technology-into-space/
Martinis, J. M. (2015). Qubit metrology for building a fault-tolerant quantum computer. *npj Quantum Information, 1*(1), 1–3.
Millington-Smith, D. (2023). A quantum solution to quantification: Industrial deployment of quantum gas lidar camera for continuous, autonomous monitoring and quantification of methane emissions. https://doi.org/10.1038/nature19797.7.
Milner, G. (2017). *Pinpoint—How GPS is changing technology, culture, and our minds*. W.W. Norton and Company.
Padgett, M. J., & Boyd, R. W. (2017). An introduction to ghost imaging: Quantum and classical. *Philosophical Transactions of the Royal Society, A, 375*, 20160233.
QLMtec.com. (2024). QLM. Retrieved May 14, 2024, from https://www.qlmtec.com/solution/
QT-PRI. (2023). https://www.qt-pri.org/
QuantIC. (2022). https://quantic.ac.uk/media/Media_1054871_smxx.pdf
QuantIC. (2024). *3D imaging of stationary and moving objects in turbid underwater environments*. https://www.quantic.ac.uk/technologies/underwater/
Quantumsensors.org. (2018). *Quantum research leads to first wearable brain scanner*. https://www.quantumsensors.org/news/2018/04/09/quantum-research-leads-to-first-wearable-brain-scanner-2
Quantumsensors.org. (2022). *UK quantum technology hub sensors and timing researcher creates*. Retrieved July 1, 2021, from https://www.quantumsensors.org/
QuantX. (2023). *QuantX labs and SSTL partner to propel Australian quantum clock technology into space*. https://quantxlabs.com/quantx-labs-and-sstl-partner-to-propel-australian-quantum-clock-technology-into-space/
RTS International. (2019). Economic benefits of the Global positioning system (GPS), June.

Stray, B., et al. (2022). Quantum sensing for gravity cartography. *Nature, 602*, 590–594. https://doi.org/10.1038/s41586-021-04315-3

Templier, S. et al. (2022). Tracking the vector acceleration with a hybrid quantum accelerometer triad. *Science Advances*, *8*(45).

Tralli, D. M., Blom, R. G., Zlotnicki, V., Donnellan, A., & Evans, D. L. (2005). Satellite remote sensing of earthquake, volcano, flood, landslide and coastal inundation hazards. *ISPRS Journal of Photogrammetry and Remote Sensing, 59*(4), 185–198.

Wired. (2024). The dangerous rise of GPS attacks, 30 April https://www.wired.com/story/the-dangerous-rise-of-gps-attacks/

Wright, M. J., et al. (2022). Cold atom inertial sensors for navigation applications. *Frontiers in Physics, 10*, Article 994459.

CHAPTER 5

Summary and Conclusions

This chapter covers:

- *A discussion of how quantum technologies from different application areas may integrate with one another to create radically new customer value propositions, business models, and industrial architectures;*
- *Policy considerations across different countries, and comments on responsible innovation;*
- *A discussion of some of the philosophical aspects of quantum mechanics, and how these might apply to business model developments;*
- *Concluding thoughts.*

Introduction

It is well known that complex phenomena emerge from the interactions of sub-modules in often unexpected ways (Theise, 2023). For example, in the Game of Life, mathematician John Conway shows the emergence of sometimes surprisingly complex patterns from simple rules of interactions between living and dead cells in two-dimensional grid squares. Digital computers and related digital technologies have come together in unexpected ways to create a complex system. For example, digital computers were initially used to convert manual processes into digital formats in the manufacturing industry. This led to further development of product varieties, as it was possible to create more personalised versions

C. Velu et al., *The Business of Quantum Technologies*,
https://doi.org/10.1007/978-3-031-99808-9_5

of products based on customer needs. Such product variety demanded more sophisticated new product-development methods, such as the use of computer-aided design technologies (Cortada, 2004). The subsequent iteration was the embedding of sensors in the product to collect data about product usage, which enabled better advice on the optimal use of the product. For example, in the earth-moving equipment market, tractors had embedded sensors, which enabled the original equipment manufacturers to provide value-added advice to farmers on how to optimise the use of the tractors and related farm equipment. Once connected, they can be integrated into other platform-based systems, including weather, irrigation, and crop management, to build a system of systems (Porter & Hepplemann, 2015). Such systems could leverage state-of-the-art artificial intelligence and machine-learning algorithms to provide advice to farmers on the end-to-end process of farming, from planting and harvesting to sales and distribution. These new customer value propositions will enable new business models to emerge, as well as enabling changes in the industrial architecture, combining digital computers and related digital technologies, including the internet. We believe that a similar complex new industrial architecture will emerge from combining quantum technology uses.

First, in this chapter, we sketch a scenario describing how such quantum technology combinations might create a new industrial landscape. So far, we have looked at individual quantum technologies, but we have not described how they might integrate with one another to provide societal benefit. In this chapter, we imagine a future smart quantum city and consider how a range of quantum technologies might work in parallel to support transport.

Second, we explore how industrial policies might influence the development of such a future, and how the meaning attributed to quantum technologies might influence the outcome. We will also take an international perspective on policies supporting quantum technology development. And, third, we will explore how quantum technologies need to be developed responsibly to benefit all parts of society.

Finally, we will look at some of the philosophical aspects of quantum science that may act as blockers to understanding, thereby limiting the industrial take-up of quantum technologies, with reference to how developing new business models might help to overcome this issue.

Bringing Quantum Technologies Together

We have now introduced several emerging quantum technologies that individually hold the potential to transform society in many ways. We might conclude with a vision that several of these cutting-edge quantum technologies could work in parallel, holistically, seamlessly integrating with classical systems to revolutionise the way we might live in a "quantum city".

Let us imagine such a smart quantum city (SQC), where we are surrounded by advanced autonomous vehicles, terrestrial and airborne, that have to navigate a complex environment, and thus need to be managed and coordinated to ensure their reliability and performance. Here, integrating quantum computing, quantum communication, quantum sensing, navigation, and timing is very beneficial in creating a smarter, safer, more resilient quantum city.

Autonomous vehicles such as drones, trains, and road vehicles will navigate in complex, dynamic scenarios, involving re-routing, changing traffic densities, and links between transport modes. Such complexity brings challenges in how to effectively coordinate these vehicles as they operate in the real world. In the SQC, hybrid classical—quantum computing could enable these vehicles to optimise their routes, simulating complex traffic scenarios and efficiently processing data on road conditions, vehicle interactions, traffic signals, and driver behaviours. In addition, quantum computing could help to identify, plan, and schedule the best traffic routes with high efficiency, accuracy, and safety.

This will need a robust data integrity system, with full security on the data exchanged between different vehicles, and between vehicles and other infrastructure. In the SQC, quantum communication technologies could allow autonomous vehicles to share encryption keys confidentially when communicating with controllers, or with other vehicles, providing resilience to attack by bad actors.

To ensure safety, autonomous vehicles also need high-precision measurements of their locations and environmental surroundings. Quantum sensors could detect objects such as other vehicles, pedestrians, cyclists, or obstacles, even under harsh environmental conditions such as fog or low light visibility, reducing the likelihood of traffic collisions. In addition, quantum sensors could be embedded in continuous monitoring infrastructure, providing vehicles with real-time updates on traffic conditions.

The SQC will require accurate and stable time synchronisation between vehicles and traffic system infrastructure, potentially provided by quantum clocks. Quantum timing will also be used as part of GPS systems. Moreover, autonomous drones will need very tight lane-management systems, which might be enabled by quantum-based position, navigation, and timing systems.

Quantum technologies could also help where a combination of electricity and hydrogen-based fuels is used in autonomous vehicles, and quantum clocks could provide the precise timing needed to distribute electricity, while hydrogen-based vehicles might use a sensing & imaging system to detect hydrogen leaks.

In short, these quantum technologies working synergistically in the SQC may be important in applications such as autonomous vehicle management (see Fig. 5.1). However, as indicated in previous chapters, such an SQC would require technical and societal innovation at multiple levels. Challenges and issues remain in, for instance, the technical development of these quantum technologies, the integration between quantum and legacy systems, organisational implementation and adoption, and supply chain interactions. We thus encourage research from multiple disciplines to work on the business of quantum technologies, bearing in mind a vision of the smart quantum city.

The Transition to Quantum

One starting point to fulfil the vision of the smart quantum city is to effectively understand how to migrate society from the current classical systems to quantum-embedded hybrid systems. As suggested in previous chapters, quantum technologies will not necessarily work alone; they will generally need to integrate with conventional legacy systems. In the short-term vision of the quantum city, there is likely to be a phase where digital technologies transition to quantum–digital hybrid technologies. This will require the development of a quantum-based technology roadmap, covering strategic alignment within and across organisations, integration of horizontal and vertical systems, development of key performance metrics, and synchronisation between innovation practices and strategic objectives (Phaal, 2024; Vinayavekhin & Phaal, 2023).

First, the functions of quantum technologies might need to be aligned with quantum product development to address why quantum technologies are demanded, how they are supplied, and what products are

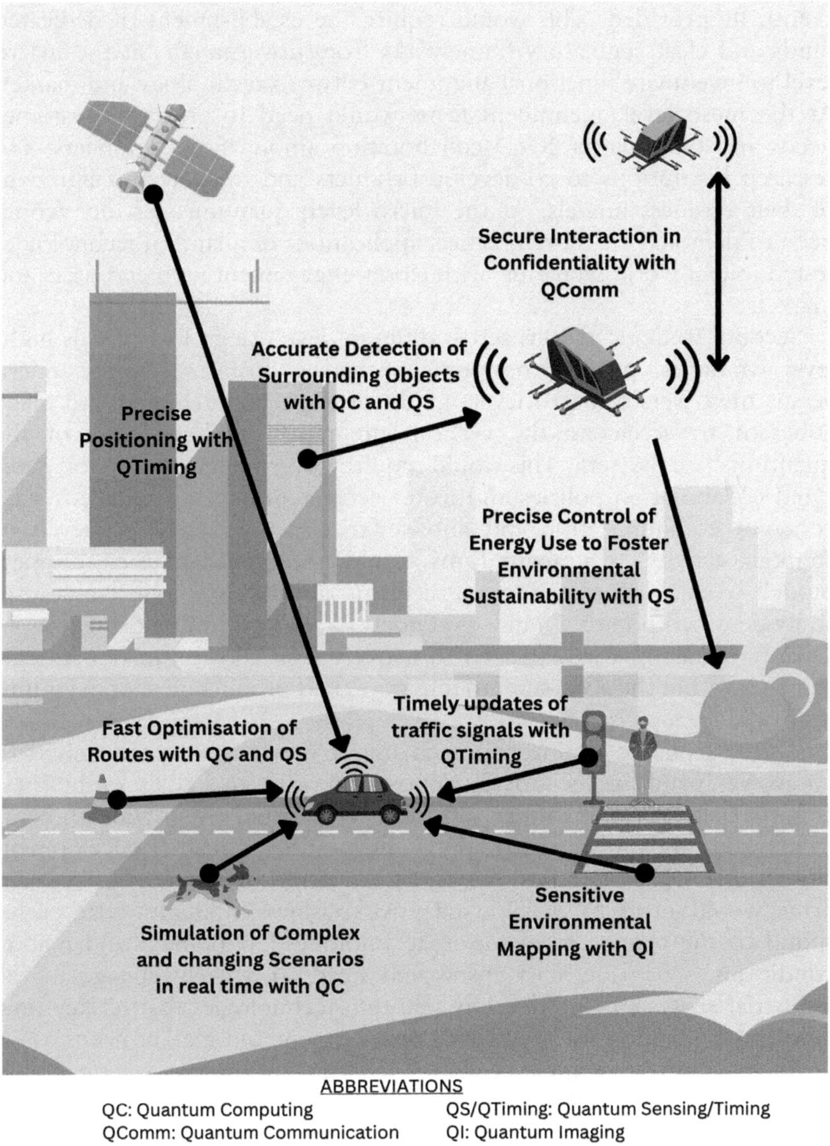

Fig. 5.1 Autonomous vehicles in an envisioned quantum city

eventually provided. This would require the establishment of dedicated funds and clear regulatory frameworks from governments at the macro level to incentivise functional alignment between technology and market. At the meso level, incumbent firms would need to prioritise customer needs and build closer R&D collaboration among firms, suppliers, and research institutions to co-develop products and mitigate misalignment of their business models. At the micro level, quantum start-ups would need to demonstrate more practical applications of quantum technologies tested in real-world scenarios, with closer engagement with end users and markets.

Second, strategic actions across different levels (e.g., low- versus high-level strategies, product development versus business strategy, micro versus meso versus macro level) might need to be integrated and made coherent to accelerate the vertical integration of knowledge of the quantum-based system. This would require governments to develop dedicated collaboration policies and foster ecosystem development, ensuring coherent communication and knowledge exchange across all levels of strategic activity. Incumbent firms would need to adapt their business models to establish cross-functional teams and develop holistic quantum strategies, incorporating multi-level goals for vertical strategic integration. Quantum start-ups would need to actively seek and formulate strategic alliances within the ecosystem to integrate their product development into industrial legacy systems.

Third, a phased timing approach might need to be synchronised to co-evolve quantum technology innovation with the goals of business commercialisation and societal diffusion. This would require governments to allocate funds in a phased approach, monitor industrial development closely, and review or adjust relevant policies in a timely way. Incumbent firms would need to develop adaptive business strategies that correspond to the change in quantum technology development and market conditions. Quantum start-ups would need to actively engage in the industrial ecosystem and develop quantum technologies that hit key time milestones, aligning with industrial development and market needs.

Such system-level thinking about quantum technology roadmapping, interpreted within the integrated multi-level and business model perspective, allows us to conceptualise how the quantum industry is realised, using Phaal et al.'s (2011) industry emergence framework, shown in Fig. 5.2.

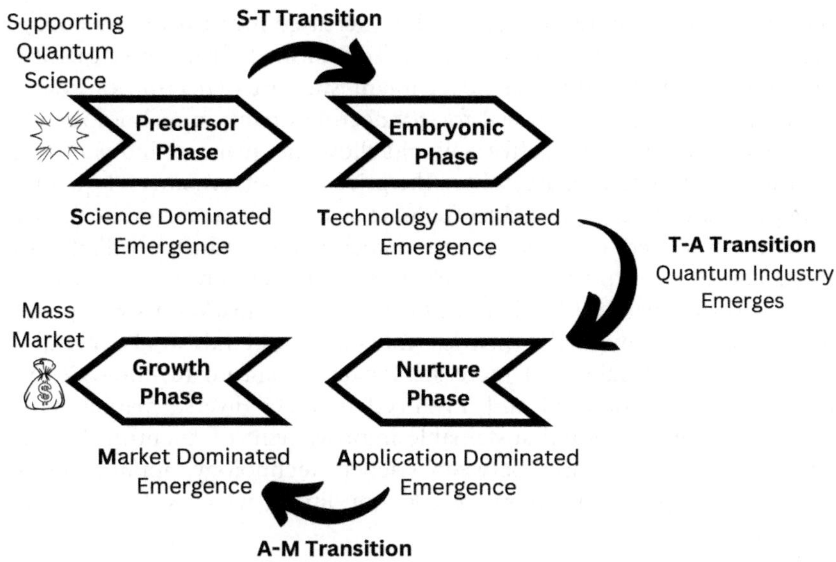

Fig. 5.2 Industrial emergence framework (adapted from Phaal et al., 2011)

Over the last 20 years, the quantum industry has experienced the precursor and embryonic phases in Phaal's model. At the precursor phase, the quantum industry was establishing its supporting applied scientific demonstrators, where quantum science informed quantum technology application potential, and stimulated industrial and market interest for investment and feasibility testing. This was followed by a science-to-technology (S-T) transition phase, where the feasibility of quantum technologies was demonstrated in principle, supporting the emergence and demonstration of application-specific functional quantum technologies in industry. By dedicated improvement of the reliability and performance of quantum technologies, a technology-dominated quantum industry emerges, during which market-directed quantum technology applications would be demonstrated in industry.

The quantum industry is emerging from its transition phase, moving from technology-dominated to application-dominated industry (T–A). More commercial potential of quantum technologies is being unlocked and demonstrated through firms' revenue generation. Quantum economic advantage and value capture are being showcased, stimulating the emergence of more market interest, increased investment and engagement of start-ups, the movement of established firms into quantum technologies, and additional government support. The role of systems integrators is becoming crucial for connecting quantum technology with commercialisation. These efforts would allow the quantum industry to be nurtured into its next phase, where the price and performance of quantum applications will be improved to facilitate sustainable quantum businesses.

It is envisioned that the quantum technology industry will demonstrate and grow into the mass market over the next phases (typically the application-to-market (A–M) transition phase and market growth phase), where market-dominated industries will emerge and industrial demand for quantum technologies will increase. Finally, quantum technologies will have sufficiently matured and advanced to meet diverse market needs, leading to the steady and sustainable improvement of quantum business and industry. The phases between science, technology, application and market development are iterative and non-linear, which will have policy implications.

Policy Considerations

Countries have taken significantly different approaches to their support of quantum, with some preferring a non-interventionist approach to let industry develop the technologies with ad hoc support for academia. Others, meanwhile, have dedicated programmes, strategies, missions and funding, influencing at a higher level. The extent of these efforts varies significantly, as does their organisation, with some sitting at local or state level, while others are large-scale endeavours coordinated at national level. Below are some examples of the different approaches taken by countries and their potential effects.

The UK has had a National Quantum Technologies Programme since 2014, the first of its kind worldwide, beginning with the creation of four academically led hubs, encompassing the leading research groups in quantum technologies across the UK. It is noteworthy that, in quantum computing, the hub has operated across the stack and without narrowing down on a particular hardware modality, indicating the desire to maintain a broad capability at this stage. Together with the later-established National Quantum Computing Centre, the hubs represent the core of a rich country-wide ecosystem in the UK, supporting a network of over fifty quantum technology start-ups. The phased government support of commercialising quantum technologies in the UK—primarily through Innovate UK—has supported and grown these start-ups, combined with venture capital investment. The UK's National Quantum Strategy is continuing much of this effort, while five missions (GOV.UK, 2024a) are focusing on achieving specified objectives that will have significant spill-over benefit. The UK government describes such mission-oriented innovation as dating back to the Longitude Act of 1714, which incentivised innovators to develop methods for determining longitude to assist navigation at sea, and led to huge improvements in marine chronometers, lunar distance tables, and more. The ambition is for these missions to act as a focal point for both academia and industry in the UK.

The European Union launched its Quantum Flagship programme in 2018. This is a large-scale, long-term research initiative with a budget of €1 billion. Its primary goal is to consolidate and expand European scientific leadership in quantum technologies. It has developed a quantum strategic research agenda (European Commission, 2020), including quantum communications, computing, simulation, and sensing and metrology. These four areas are anchored by a common basis in basic science and supported by work in cross-cutting areas such as engineering, education, and training.

Australia too has a National Quantum Strategy, published in 2023 (GOV.AU, 2023). Much of Australia's governance and R&D funding sits at state level, and there is clear recognition of this within the strategy. The individual capabilities and efforts of the various states within Australia are highlighted, with an ambition to coordinate a national effort to ensure these are aligned and complementary. In quantum computing, it is notable that Australia has recently focused many of its resources around one company—PSIQuantum—an American company that will build and operate successive generations of its quantum computers in Brisbane, following A$940 million of investment from both the federal government and the state of Queensland. Developing an ecosystem around one organisation stands in contrast to the UK, possibly leading to a cluster of quantum technology organisations in Brisbane and the surrounding areas.

The USA passed its National Quantum Initiative Act in 2018, with a large focus on R&D through its NSF and DoE national labs. The act allocated $1.2 billion, although there is also regional development funding (e.g., UTNews, 2024). However, the USA has by far the largest private sector, with companies such as IBM, Google, and Amazon investing heavily in quantum; private investment in the USA is significant, estimated at over 13 times that of China (QuantumInsider, 2023). It is worth noting that the USA has a rich history of supporting private enterprise through government procurement, particularly through defence, and the National Defense Authorization Act (NDAA) may mean the DOD has increased activity in quantum technologies going forwards. Finally, the 2022 Memorandum issued by the White House to all federal agencies, providing instruction on migrating to post-quantum cryptography, showcases a meso-level change directed by the government, with entities who work with these agencies expected to comply with the new directive (NSM-10, 2022).

The broader topic of regulation around quantum technologies is an ongoing discussion, and one that is likely to intensify as these technologies advance. Regulation can stifle or promote change, can shift the pathway a technology takes, and—if insufficient—can expose the wider public to risk (Wiener, 2004). It is perhaps the most obvious example of the regime level referred to in Chapter 1. A recent report by the UK's Regulatory Horizons Council noted that it was "too early to jump to legally based regulation given the nascency of many quantum technologies" (GOV.UK, 2024b). Nevertheless, the report also notes the key for early regulatory discussions and the need for businesses to plan long term. The UK has described its position on regulating quantum technologies as pro-innovation, a stance that it and countries such as Singapore have previously adopted with emerging technologies, including AI. The model seeks to balance public interests with commercial agendas (Lim & Chng, 2024).

Given the potentially transformative impact of quantum technologies, both good and bad, it remains to be seen whether most countries will take a similar view, and the impact this may have. A key factor may be introducing regulations on the technologies themselves, or revising regulations in application areas, for instance, updating financial trading regulations given the potential greater capabilities of quantum computers and atomic clocks. Regulations around quantum communications are likely to be concerned with security of information; similarly, regulations may be needed around data privacy in quantum sensing and imaging. While many states already have regulations in those broad areas, they are likely to need to evolve as the technology drives the art of the possible.

There are, of course, many examples of firms behaving in ways that go against the letter or the spirit of regulations. For instance, in 2015, the US

Environmental Protection Agency discovered that Volkswagen had been selling cars with a software "defeat device" that could detect when they were being tested for regulated environmental emissions, and they could adjust the performance accordingly to improve the test results (Crête, 2016). Similarly, failures in regulation of the financial services sector in 2008 led to the global financial crisis—Velu (2024) has explored the external risks of a lack of consumer protection in this context in relation to *conduct risk* as a result of information asymmetry and conflicts of interest. Conduct risk was defined by the Financial Services Authority in 2011 as "the risk that firm behaviour will result in poor outcomes for customers". Regulations should exist to ensure that consumers of a product or service are treated fairly. As per the National Audit Office, regulation should "protect and benefit people, businesses and the environment" and "support economic growth". Hence, the objective is to develop a culture within firms to act in way that is fair to customers and markets and to ask whether a practice "should" be adopted as opposed to whether it "could" be done within the existing regulatory framework.

In the digital sector, Birkinshaw describes how digital firms often challenge existing norms and regulations (Birkinshaw, 2024). Birkinshaw categorises three ways in which firms can use tactics to work around established regulations:

- The finesse approach, where firms find gaps in the existing regulations and exploit these gaps and their inconsistencies;
- The sidestep approach, where firms argue that the regulations do not apply to their business; and
- The nullify approach, where firms act freely by completely denying the existence of an a priori market and corresponding regulations.

Many of the points made in Birkinshaw's analysis are likely to apply to quantum companies and their customers. For example, it is possible that some quantum technology firms (or their customers) sidestep regulations, potentially leading to adverse societal impacts. Given the capital-intensive nature of their investments, quantum firms may challenge traditional competition rules, leading to monopolistic practices. Such dominance could reduce competition, resulting in higher prices, fewer choices, and stifled innovation. Similarly, quantum technology could be used in ways that breach ethical standards, for example, in surveillance or military applications. Hence, regulators should be mindful of developing appropriate responses to such rule-bending, as well as developing frameworks to enable appropriate institutional innovation to stay ahead of firms' practices as they develop new business models for the quantum-enabled economy.

In the context of quantum technology, the regulatory landscape has not yet stabilised regarding both the quantum technology and its associated products, or the processes associated with these technologies (UK Regulatory Horizons Council, 2024). It is therefore essential for government or regulatory institutions to provide adequate guidance to quantum firms, which may range from granting "light-touch" recommendations and best practice to implementing stringent controls. A dynamic, negotiated, flexible, and adaptable approach is crucial to ensuring that quantum technology innovation flourishes and co-evolves with regulatory practices while public interests are safeguarded (Birkinshaw, 2024; Perrier, 2022; UK Regulatory Horizons Council, 2024), particularly now that quantum firms are defining the legal status of their products, which could cultivate new regulation and benchmarking policies. Regulators must be actively involved in the ecosystem to balance firms' business model innovation advantages without damaging public welfare. Institutional innovation will also need to keep pace with the rapid advancement of quantum technology, ensuring that regulations support growth without stifling emerging business models.

Responsible Research

Regulations aside, many countries are considering the wider moral and ethical questions around developing quantum technologies. Quantum technologies are likely to have long-lasting impacts on society, and it is important to have a considered and ethical approach to researching and developing these technologies that looks at any potential social issues. *Responsible research and innovation* (RRI) means undertaking research in a way that anticipates how it might affect people and the environment in the future, so that we can gain the most benefit and avoid harm.

For example, in the UK, RRI was part of the National Quantum Technologies Programme from its inception. This work led to a *Responsible Research and Innovation Landscape Report* (Ingelsant et al., 2016), which suggested a framework for a tailored RRI process. This report emphasised the role of the public in technology development, stating that "...dialogue with the public, with early adopters, with civil society, and other stakeholders is crucial to ensure that the research delivers results which will be widely recognised and welcomed". Further work between the same team and consultancy firm EY considered responsible quantum computing communications (Ten Holter et al., 2024). The aim was to: (1) address perceived gaps in cross-departmental communication within policy-making teams and departments, (2) facilitate and support ongoing public dialogue and awareness, and (3) deploy responsible, innovation-based translational frameworks for quantum spin-outs into industrial or commercial contexts. Key recommendations from the work included:

- Managing expectations around time frames for quantum computing at scale and proceeding with caution when discussing potential capabilities and limitations;
- Continuing to foreground equitable access to quantum computing resources, infrastructure and talent, to advance global responses and collaboration;
- Developing more nuanced approaches to the competitive nature of quantum, to address capacity issues and mitigate digital divides within and between nations;
- Leveraging governmental capacity for absorbing risk, building markets, shaping governance, and levelling the playing field within and between nations; and
- Recognising that developing this new technology is a marathon, not a sprint, and that treating it like the "space race" may hinder overall progress.

Philosophical Aspects

Business models could be conceptualised as a cognitive instrument that acts as a bridge between technology and the market. Technologies capture the ongoing combinatorial evolution of knowledge of natural phenomena and harness this for a particular useful purpose (Arthur, 2010). Markets capture the ongoing combinatorial evolution of institutions and social relations, enabling parties to engage in an exchange (Fligstein, 1996). The business model then articulates expectations and visions among actors, describing how the value of quantum technologies could be created and captured. Moreover, business models emphasise the customer-centric focus on problem-solving. Such an approach helps to overcome cognitive biases among scientists and engineers by focusing on external validation rather than emphasising the properties of the technology. In so doing, the business model serves as a reference language and enables collective sense-making (Bidmon & Knab, 2018) on the application of quantum technologies. Hence, business models could link quantum technologies to broader stakeholders, allowing markets and user preferences to support the attraction of funding and eventual adoption of these technologies. Therefore, understanding the philosophical views of quantum mechanics might be important in terms of how the technology is perceived by scientists, engineers, and business managers, which could influence the development of business models.

Quantum technologies are often seen as enigmatic and difficult to grasp. This perception may stem primarily from the nature of quantum mechanics, which deviates significantly from classical physics. There are profound philosophical differences between interpretations of quantum mechanics, which contributes to this complexity (Barad, 2013; Loewer, 1998; Schwartz et al., 2005).

Interpretations of Quantum Mechanics

Let us examine a few ways of interpreting quantum mechanics, with a view to highlighting this complexity. One of the fundamental issues with "explaining" quantum mechanics is demonstrated by what has become known as the measurement problem. As described in earlier chapters, a quantum object has a state, and the state is generally a superposition of all possible quantum states for that object. However, when we measure the quantum state, we *never* find the object in that superposition—rather, when measured, the state updates to just one of the possible allowed states. Recall our analogy with spinning coins: when we catch the coin, we only ever observe heads or tails, never a superposition of both.

However, quantum mechanical objects are not spinning coins. An atomic nucleus is a quantum mechanical object, so how are we to understand, for example, nuclear processes such as radioactive decay as quantum mechanical processes? Unlike the tossed coin, the nucleus might never interact with an experimenter, and yet presumably it will decay at some point, regardless of whether an observer is present. Schrödinger's famous cat thought experiment emphasises this point. The cat is held in a sealed box, with a vial of lethal poison, triggered to break open when a radioactive nucleus decays. While the box is sealed, the nucleus is described by quantum mechanics as being in a superposition of "decayed and not decayed". Without opening the box, how should we describe the state of the cat? As being in a superposition of "dead and not dead" simultaneously? According to Schrödinger, this is nonsense—cats are either alive or dead, never in a superposition of both, regardless of whether their "cat state" has been measured, in this case by opening the box. What, then, is a measurement of a quantum state, and where is the cut-off (if any) between quantum measurements and classical observations?

Furthermore, let us consider Heisenberg's well-known uncertainty principle, developed from purely mathematical principles. This sets a fundamental limit on the amount of information we can obtain from measuring a quantum mechanical object. Specifically, there are strict mathematical limits on how precisely we can know some properties of a quantum mechanical object simultaneously. For example, if we know the position of an object very accurately, there is a strict limit on how accurately we can know its momentum. Conversely, if we know the momentum very accurately, there is the same strict limit on how accurately we can know its position. As an analogy, consider measuring the velocity of a car using a radar gun. The signal emitted by the radar gun in principle has no effect on the velocity of the car—it merely measures what that velocity is. However, using a radar gun to measure the velocity of an atom is very different: for even the most glancing interaction between the radar signal and the atom, we end up affecting the velocity of the atom, or its position, or both. Heisenberg's uncertainty principle has a precise, mathematical formulation, and it follows on from the logic of how mathematical entities in quantum mechanics relate to one another, but it is experimentally verifiable. We emphasise that this is not just because we have not built sufficiently accurate detectors, but a direct consequence of the mathematical logic of quantum mechanics.

How do we interpret these related issues of measurement, with the uncertainty principle apparently showing us that nature has an inherent "fuzziness" that we can never overcome, and with the measurement problem saying, in addition to this fuzziness, that when we make a measurement we only ever observe a definite state, despite quantum mechanics being built on the principles of superpositions of states? Are the quantum states truly fundamental, or do they represent our knowledge of a quantum system? Over the last century there have been several interpretations of this issue but potentially no clear-cut way of experimentally testing which interpretation corresponds to reality.

The Copenhagen Interpretation

The most radical departure of quantum mechanics from classical physics, based on one school of thought, is that it is the introduction of human agency in influencing what—and when—to measure that determines the outcome and subsequent measurements. There was a disagreement between Heisenberg and Bohr about the meaning of the uncertainty principle. Karan Barad outlines this disagreement in her book *Meeting the Universe Halfway* (Barad, 2007). Heisenberg's interpretation was epistemic, based on not being able to measure the position and momentum simultaneously because of the nature of the disturbances that measuring one construct causes for the other—the uncertainty principle (Barad, 2007). Bohr, on the other hand, argued that it is because of the nature of the set-up of the instrument for measurement: if one were to measure the position, the instrument would need to be static, but to measure momentum the instrument would need to be moveable, and one cannot do both at the same time. In this sense, the measurement issue is ontic (ontological)—the indeterminacy principle (Barad, 2007). Hence, the cut—which came to be known as the Heisenberg cut—between the subject (the knower or agent of observation) and object of observation (knowledge) is not predetermined but based on what is being measured (von Neumann, 1955).

There has been significant scientific and philosophical discussion about the topic since the exchange between Bohr and Heisenberg on the limitations of measurement apparatus and disturbances from measurements, respectively (Atkinson & Peijnenburg, 2022; Hilgevoord & Uffink, 2024). For example, there have been major advancements in the capabilities of the apparatus used for measurement and also ongoing discussion about the definition of uncertainty. Despite these developments, everyday language based on classical conceptions of the world, describing a moment-by-moment account of "what is happening", is limiting when it comes to quantum mechanical formalism, at least in Bohr's interpretation. In Bohr's view, quantum mechanics does not tell us what is happening—only what one is likely to find if we look to find out (Werner & Farrelly, 2019). Therefore, the quest to clarify our understanding of the quantum mechanical principles and the associated measurement uncertainty continues from a philosophical standpoint (Hilgevoord & Uffink, 2024).

Bohr's interpretation came to be known as the Copenhagen interpretation (CQM). CQM posits that the quantum state of a system is its complete physical state, with some properties having determinate values and others not. Based on this interpretation, sub-atomic particles do not possess determinate trajectories.

Bohmian Mechanics (Pilot Wave Theory)

Conversely, Bohmian mechanics (BQM), advocated by David Bohm, maintains that particles always have definite positions and trajectories. BQM posits that the evolution of the quantum state and particle positions is deterministic, governed by the Schrödinger equation and a "guidance equation", respectively (Schwartz et al., 2005). The probabilities calculated from the Schrödinger equation represent ignorance of the precise value of the quantum state, such as the position and momentum, because of some "hidden" variable (Loewer, 1998).

The Many Worlds Interpretation

Following Everett (1957), several authors have interpreted quantum mechanics as implying that *everything* in the universe is quantum. In this view, there is no "cut" between the quantum and classical worlds, and measurement is merely another quantum mechanical transformation, but crucially, the measurer (observer) is also a quantum mechanical system that becomes entangled with the quantum state being observed. Measurement in many worlds does not "collapse" a superposition; rather, every possible state that the superposition could be measured to be in continues to evolve in diverging, parallel universes (hence the "many worlds" moniker).

Spontaneous Collapse Theories

Spontaneous collapse (e.g., Ghirardi et al., 1986) describes quantum objects as dropping out of their general superposition state into a definite state of their own accord, independently of an observer performing a measurement. Proponents of this interpretation claim that it explains both quantum mechanics at small scales and classical physics at macroscopic scales, without requiring a special role for the observer.

Other Interpretations

There are many other interpretations of quantum mechanics, with each one placing more or less emphasis on the role of the observer with relation to the quantum system. In some, the observer is central to the interpretation, with the quantum state becoming a purely epistemic description of the observer's beliefs about the system (Fuchs & Shack, 2013). In others, while the observer remains central to the interpretation, the state itself remains a real, ontic entity, and its updating from a superposition to a single definite state when measured is somehow caused by the observer's consciousness (Stapp, 2001). Some interpretations are deterministic, and some feature hidden variables. In some, the universe itself is described by a quantum state.

These varying explanations of quantum mechanics highlight important philosophical differences. For example, the Copenhagen interpretation (CQM) involves indeterminacy and suggests a mind-dependent reality, while Bohmian mechanics (BQM) maintains determinism and a realist perspective. CQM posits that the unobservable reality is beyond our understanding, whereas BQM provides a consistent account of this reality, supporting a more objective view. This dichotomy underscores the philosophical challenges of quantum mechanics, potentially complicating the adoption of quantum technologies.

In classical physics, cause and effect are straightforward and external, making technology easier to understand and communicate. However, in some interpretations of quantum mechanics, the observer becomes an active part of the causal chain, influencing what—and when—measurements are made, which impacts subsequent measurements. This implies that human agency plays a crucial role in determining outcomes, making quantum mechanics difficult to understand for those who are used to clear, external causes (Barad, 2013). In this view, each action by a human agent is a preparation expected to produce an experiential response or feedback—the conscious choices of human agents are non-trivially included in the causal interpretation of science, especially in decision-making and attention-focusing tasks, even bringing a critical part of scientific investigation on how we probe nature directly into the causal structure. Thus, in this interpretation, quantum theory provides a framework where mental efforts and conscious choices are causally effective.

Consequently, understanding quantum technologies requires a more integrated understanding of both quantum mechanics and its philosophical underpinnings. In classical physics, technology can be treated as a black box, but quantum mechanics may necessitate an awareness of how observer actions and internal experiences, at least indirectly, form part of the causal chain that influences the system. For example, classical physics describes the external world without reference to human thoughts, while some interpretations of quantum mechanics involve describing both the activities of knowledge-seeking agents and the knowledge they acquire.

The enigmatic nature of quantum mechanics, with its potential counter-intuitive observer dependence, and the philosophical debates surrounding its interpretations, may present challenges for the adoption of quantum technologies. Often, engineers and business managers can leave the technology somewhat "under the hood". Such an arm's-length approach might not be appropriate in the case of quantum technologies. These complexities require a deeper understanding and a shift in perspective, ultimately impacting the communication and integration of quantum solutions in practical applications. Hence, there should be a concerted effort to solve these cognitive challenges.

Business models could be a powerful framework to ease cognitive burden in the adoption of quantum technologies. Business models can be used as cognitive instruments that embody the understanding of causal links between the material exchange mechanisms of organisations and their environments that exist in managers' cognition (Baden-Fuller & Mangematin, 2013). Business models can mitigate cognitive barriers to innovation by providing structured frameworks and processes that guide decision-making, reduce uncertainty, and promote a more objective evaluation of the opportunities and risks (Baden-Fuller & Morgan, 2010). Understanding how the material properties affect the socio-economic outcomes through the design of business models requires further investigation (Orlikowski, 2007).

Conclusions

This book is, of course, written at a time when massive developments are occurring in quantum technologies. Globally, more money is being invested in Quantum 2.0 than ever before, and every year new quantum technologies are appearing on the market. While there is currently no fully fault-tolerant quantum computer, firms are positioning roadmaps to fault tolerance with increased confidence. Quantum sensing and imaging firms are moving from prototypes to scalable products, with pathways emerging for medical regulatory approval in healthcare applications, increasing miniaturisation for transport needs and improving accuracy for navigation. Post-quantum security protocols are being discussed, and the first quantum-enabled networks are being constructed. Governments are setting "grand challenges" to which quantum technologies are likely to contribute and creating multi-year programmes to support quantum technologies moving into the marketplace.

Nonetheless, we ask: Is industry ready for the changes that quantum technologies will bring? In Chapter 1, we described a framework for thinking about the broader changes that industry needs to prepare for in light of technological disruptions, involving changes at the landscape (macro), regime (meso), and niche (micro) levels. We also looked at how interactions between these levels enable the adoption of new technologies and drive change in business models. In subsequent chapters we looked at some case-study vignettes of developments in the quantum technology marketplace, and how new firms are positioning their technologies at the micro level. We also considered how governments are putting strategies in place that will enable quantum technology development at the macro level. If there is a gap, it is potentially at the meso level. Incumbents are exploring quantum technology, but for most firms, it is far from mainstream business. As we discussed in Chapter 1, digital computing saw a decline in productivity for several years as the technology became a reality in industry, before productivity rose again in later years. Industrialists need to look at the micro and macro states and think hard about how their businesses will need to change in the coming Quantum 2.0 Revolution.

The challenge for incumbents, start-ups, and policy-makers alike is to build a vision of a new world, where different applications of quantum technologies come together to make the world a better place. We need a framework to envision such a future state and a roadmap to achieve it, in a way that is fair and responsible, so that all parts of society can benefit. In doing so, we believe the way that industrial policy is created, and the perception of what quantum mechanics is, will influence the trajectory of the innovation and the business model development. We hope this book provides the scaffolding for us to jointly build a better quantum-enabled world.

References

Arthur, W. B. (2010). *The nature of technology: What it is and how it evolves*. Penguin UK.

Atkinson, D., & Peijnenburg, J. (2022). How uncertain is Heisenberg's uncertainty principle? *HOPOS: The Journal of the International Society for the History and Philosophy of Science, 12*(1), 1–21.

Baden-Fuller, C., & Morgan, M. S. (2010). Business models as models. *Long Range Planning, 43*(2–3), 156–171. https://doi.org/10.1016/j.lrp.2010.02.005

Baden-Fuller, C., & Mangematin, V. (2013). Business models: A challenging agenda. *Strategic Organization, 11*(4), 418–427. https://doi.org/10.1177/1476127013510112

Barad, K. (2007). *Meeting the universe halfway: Quantum physics and the entanglement of matter and meaning*. Duke University Press.

Barad, K. (2013). Posthumanist performativity: Toward an understanding of how matter comes to matter. *Women, Science, and Technology: A Reader in Feminist Science Studies, 28*(3), 473–494. https://doi.org/10.4324/9780203427415-41

Bidmon, C. M., & Knab, S. F. (2018). The three roles of business models in societal transitions: New linkages between business model and transition research. *Journal of Cleaner Production, 178*, 903–916. https://doi.org/10.1016/j.jclepro.2017.12.198

Birkinshaw, J. (2024). Too Little, Too Late? How Policymakers and Regulators Respond to the Business Model Innovations of Digital Firms. *Academy of Management Perspectives, 38*(3), 269–285.

Cortada, J. W. (2004). *The digital hand: How computers changed the work of American manufacturing, transportation, and retail industries*. Oxford University Press.

Crête, R. (2016). The Volkswagen scandal from the viewpoint of corporate governance. *European Journal of Risk Regulation, 7*(1), 25–31.

European Commission. (2020). *Quantum Flagship Strategic Research Agenda*. https://ec.europa.eu/newsroom/dae/document.cfm?doc_id=65402

Everett, H. (1957). The relative state formulation of quantum mechanics. *Reviews of Modern Physics, 29*(3), 454–462.

Fligstein, F. (1996). Markets as politics: A political-cultural approach to market institutions. *American Sociological Review, 61*(4), 656–673.

Fuchs, C. A., & Shack, R. (2013). Quantum-Bayesian coherence. *Reviews of Modern Physics, 85*, 1693.

Ghirardi, G. C., Rimini, A., & Weber, T. (1986). Unified dynamics for microscopic and macroscopic systems. *Physical Review D, 34*(2), 470–491.

GOV.AU. (2023). *National Quantum Strategy*. https://www.industry.gov.au/publications/national-quantum-strategy

GOV.UK. (2024a). *National Quantum Strategy Missions*. https://www.gov.uk/government/publications/national-quantum-strategy/national-quantum-strategy-missions

GOV.UK. (2024b). *Regulating Quantum Technology Applications*. https://assets.publishing.service.gov.uk/media/65ddc83bcf7eb10015f57f9f/RHC_regulation_of_quantum_technology_applications.pdf

Hilgevoord, J., & Uffink, J. (2024). *The Uncertainty Principle, The Stanford Encyclopedia of Philosophy* (Spring Edition). In E. N. Zalta, & U. Nodelman (Eds.), https://plato.stanford.edu/entries/qt-uncertainty/#:~:text=Roughly%20speaking%2C%20the%20uncertainty%20principle,momentum%20of%20a%20physical%20system

Ingelsant, P., Hartswood, M., & Jirotka, M. (2016). Thinking Ahead to a World with Quantum Computers – The Landscape of Responsible Research and Innovation in Quantum Computing, NQIT.

Lim, S. S., & Chng, G. (2024). Verifying AI: will Singapore's experiment with AI governance set the benchmark? *Communication Research and Practice*, 1–10.

Loewer, B. (1998). Review: Copenhagen versus Bohmian Interpretations of Quantum Theory. *The British Journal for the Philosophy of Science, 49*(2), 317–328.

NSM-10 (2022). National Security Memorandum on Promoting United States Leadership in Quantum Computing While Mitigating Risks to Vulnerable Cryptographic Systems. https://www.whitehouse.gov/briefing-room/statementsreleases/2022/05/04/national-security-memorandum-on-promoting-united-states-leadership-in-quantum-computing-whilemitigating-risks-to-vulnerable-cryptographic-systems/

Orlikowski, W. J. (2007). Sociomaterial practices: Exploring technology at work. *Organization Studies, 28*(9), 1435–1448.

Perrier, E. (2022). The quantum governance stack: Models of governance for quantum information technologies. *Digital Society, 1*(3), 22.

Phaal, R. (2024). What They Should Tell You about Roadmapping at Business School. *IEEE Engineering Management Review*.

Phaal, R., O'Sullivan, E., Routley, M., Ford, S., & Probert, D. (2011). A framework for mapping industrial emergence. *Technological Forecasting and Social Change, 78*(2), 217–230.

Porter, M. E., & Heppelmann, J. E. (2015). How smart, connected products are transforming companies. *Harvard Business Review* (pp. 96–114).

QuantumInsider. (2023). *Chinese Quantum Companies and National Strategy 2023*. https://thequantuminsider.com/2023/04/13/chinese-quantum-companies-and-national-strategy-2023/

Schwartz, J. M., Stapp, H. P., & Beauregard, M. (2005). Quantum physics in neuroscience and psychology: A neurophysical model of mind-brain interaction. *Philosophical Transactions of the Royal Society B: Biological Sciences, 360*(1458), 1309–1327. https://doi.org/10.1098/rstb.2004.1598

Stapp, H. (2001). Quantum theory and the role of mind in nature. *Foundations of Physics, 31.*

Ten Holter, C., Ingelsant, P., Pijselman, M., & Jirotka, M. (2024). *Towards Responsible Quantum Computing.* https://assets.ey.com/content/dam/ey-sites/ey-com/en_uk/topics/consulting/ey_oxford_uni_whitepaper_quantum_ethics_05_2024.pdf

Theise, N. (2023). *Notes on complexity: A scientific theory of connection.* Consciousness and being. Spiegel & Grau.

UK Regulatory Horizons Council. (2024). *Regulatory Horizons Council: Regulating Quantum Technology Applications.* https://assets.publishing.service.gov.uk/media/65ddc83bcf7eb10015f57f9f/RHC_regulation_of_quantum_technology_applications.pdf#page=3.16

UTNews. (2024). *New Advanced Quantum Science Institute Will Bridge Basic Research and Applied Science.* https://news.utexas.edu/2024/04/05/new-advanced-quantum-science-institute-will-bridge-basic-research-and-applied-science/

Velu, C. (2024). *Business Model Innovation – A blueprint for strategic change.* Cambridge University Press.

Vinayavekhin, S., & Phaal, R. (2023). Roadmapping for strategic alignment, integration and synchronization. *Next generation roadmapping: Establishing technology and innovation pathways towards sustainable value* (pp. 1–24). Springer International Publishing.

von Neumann, J. (1955). *Mathematical foundations of quantum mechanics.* Princeton University Press.

Werner, R. F., & Farrelly, T. (2019). Uncertainty from Heisenberg to today. *Foundations of Physics, 49*, 460–491.

Wiener, J. B. (2004, April–August). The regulation of technology, and the technology of regulation. *Technology in Society, 26*(2–3), 483–500.

Glossary

Bit (binary digit): The fundamental unit of information in classical computing, a binary digit is a two-state system that can represent, for example, 0 or 1, false or true, heads or tails, or other binary choices. Bits can be grouped together to represent more complex data, for example, a colour image.

Classical computer: Also known as a binary or digital computer, a classical computer is one that most people are familiar with. It represents information using bits, which can be either 0 (off) or 1 (on). These bits are grouped into blocks of data that represent numbers, text, images, audio, and so on. Laptops, tablets, smartphones and digital supercomputers are all examples of classical machines.

Entanglement: Two or more quantum mechanical entities (e.g., atoms, photons, electrons) can be prepared in such a way that their combined quantum mechanical state is not fully described by the individual quantum states of the constituents. When entangled, the quantum state of each particle cannot be described independently of the state of the other particles—they are no longer individual partners but an inseparable whole for as long as the entangled state persists.

Heisenberg's uncertainty principle: Heisenberg's uncertainty principle states that it is impossible to know the values of certain pairs of physical variables to arbitrary precision. A typical example is position and momentum—the more accurately one knows one of these variables for a quantum object, the less accurately one knows the other. It gives a

C. Velu et al., *The Business of Quantum Technologies*,
https://doi.org/10.1007/978-3-031-99808-9

precise, mathematical statement of the limit to which one can, in principle, measure one variable, given the precision of one's knowledge about the other ("conjugate") variable.

Logic gate: A logic gate is a system that performs a simple, logical operation on one or more classical bits, producing a single bit as an output. An AND logic gate compares two input bits, A and B, and if both are "1", the gate outputs "1" (i.e. both input bit A AND input bit B must be "1"). An OR logic gate compares two input bits, A and B, and if either A OR B are "1", it will output "1". A NOT logic gate has only one input—if the input is "0", it will output "1", and if the input is "1" it will output "0" (i.e. it reverses the state of the input). By combining these simple logic gates, it is possible to perform more complex operations, such as addition.

Photon: A particle of light, a concept predicted by the rules of quantum mechanics and verified experimentally. Depending on the experimental conditions, photons behave as particles or waves.

PNT: Position, navigation, and timing.

Quantum state: A mathematical description of the knowledge of a quantum system. Given a quantum state, together with the rules for how the system will change over time, one has all that can, in principle, be known about that quantum system.

Qubit (quantum bit): A two-state quantum mechanical system, and the basic unit of information in a quantum computer. Since qubits are quantum mechanical objects, their state may be in a superposition (q.v.) or entangled (q.v.) with other quantum mechanical entities.

Superposition: A quantum mechanical object will generally be in a combination of all its allowed states. This general state is described as a superposition. While superposition has been experimentally verified in many situations, a direct measurement of a quantum mechanical entity never finds it in its superposition state. On the contrary, it only ever finds it in one of its bases (in this context "allowed") states, like a coin that while spinning is ***both*** heads ***and*** tails but when caught is only ever observed as heads ***or*** tails.

GPSR Compliance

The European Union's (EU) General Product Safety Regulation (GPSR) is a set of rules that requires consumer products to be safe and our obligations to ensure this.

If you have any concerns about our products, you can contact us on ProductSafety@springernature.com

In case Publisher is established outside the EU, the EU authorized representative is:

Springer Nature Customer Service Center GmbH
Europaplatz 3
69115 Heidelberg, Germany

Batch number: 10703944

Printed by Printforce, the Netherlands